Doctor Magnate

Doctor Magnate

Anil Pandey

First Printing, 2025

CONTENTS

DEDICATION

To the struggling medical student,
Who studies under dim hostel lights and still dares to dream.

To my respected seniors, inspiring juniors, and mentors —
Whose words, lives, and lessons helped shape this journey.

To the selfless government doctor,
Working without glamour but never without purpose.

And to every dreamer in a white coat,
Who wants more — not just for themselves, but for their patients, their families, and their communities.

This book is for you.

Rise with courage, prosper with ethics, and lead with purpose.
— Dr. Anil Pandey

ACKNOWLEDGMENTS

This book is not just about my journey. It's a tribute to every person who stood beside me, guided me, believed in me — and helped shape the doctor and the human being I've become.

To my **parents Aruna Shambhunath Pandey** thank you for allowing me to live life on my terms, for giving me the space to make my own decisions, and for raising me with the courage to choose an unconventional path.

To my **sister, Renu Pandey**, who first planted the seed of medicine in my mind — your inspiration set me on this path.

To my **brother Pawan Pandey**, who stood by me like a guardian throughout — your silent presence gave me confidence in every step.

To **Rishi Bhaiya**, my school senior — in the darkness of Maihar, you were the first spark of positivity. Your words and energy lit the lamp of hope when everything else seemed dim.

To **Dr. Gautam Singh** — more than a friend, you've been a mentor since 12th class. From guiding me through Indore and Bhopal to encouraging me at every critical junction, your influence has been profound.

To my **school teachers and tutors**: **R.N. Tiwari Sir**, **Tripathi Sir**, **M.P. Patel Sir**, and **Atul Garg Sir** — your classroom teachings still echo in my mind. **Kavita Pandya Ma'am**, who recognized my inner strength and encouraged me to express it. **Ranjana Shrivastav Ma'am,** whose academic support was matched by emotional and financial generosity during my most trying times. **Anurag Khare Sir**, who challenged me to break all self-imposed limits and dream beyond small-town boundaries. I am deeply thankful to **Ganesh Agrawal Sir, O. P. Tiwari Sir,** and **Ramgopal Dwivedi Sir** for their invaluable guidance and teaching.

Madhav bhaiya, Umesh bhaiya ,Arvind Gupta, and his father — for introducing me to the world of competitive exams and believing I could shine.

Sunil Mishra and his father, whose support helped me reach Allen, Kota — the real battleground of medical entrance.

To my **MBBS brothers — Abhash, Nitin, Vijay, Vishal, Pushpraj, Janardan, Bhanu, Vipin, Chandramohan (Chandu), Arun** and many more friends— thank you for being part of my journey through medical college, both in struggle and celebration.

To **Dr. Manohar Bhandari Sir**, for your guidance and belief in me when I was just starting out.

To **Dr. B.R. Parekh, Mr. Narayan Tripathi** whose timely help reminded me that compassion is the truest form of medicine.

To **Dr. Sanjay Awasiya** and **Dr. Arvind Shukla Sir**, who stood by me during one of the most turbulent chapters of my life — my accident and the ensuing legal battle. I will never forget your support and presence.

To **Dr. Sunil Rajan Sir**, thank you for introducing me to the field of orthopaedics and showing me that passion can become purpose.

To **Dr. Sanjiv Gaur Sir** and all the orthopaedic faculty members of **Gandhi Medical College, Bhopal** — you didn't just teach me orthopaedics; you taught me to become an energetic, responsible surgeon who heals with both skill and empathy.

My PG batchmates **Dr. Kripa, Dr. Yash, Dr. Dilip and Dr. Pratyush** who laughed and cried in my orthopaedic journey.

Geeta Mishra ma'am — who didn't even know me before I entered MBBS, yet when she came to know about my situation, she stood by me like my own parents and supported me in every possible way, silently and selflessly.

To my spine surgery mentors, **Dr. Amol Rege Sir** and **Dr. Sunil Nadkarni Sir**, and to all my teachers who shaped my clinical excellence in the field of spine surgery, and taught me to live with joy, gratitude, and humility.

And finally, to my **wife Karuna** and **daughter Anika**, my heart and home — your love and presence gave me strength in silence, resilience in chaos, and purpose beyond my profession.

This book would not exist without each of you. You gave me faith when I doubted myself. You stood by me when life tested me. You made me — a Doctor Magnate.

With deepest gratitude,
— **Dr. Anil Pandey**

FOREWORD

There are stories that inspire us for a moment and then there are stories that stay with us for life. The journey of Dr. Anil Pandey belongs to the latter.

Doctor Magnate is far more than an autobiography. It is the story of how gratitude, and purpose can convert even the smallest spark into a lifelong flame. Dr. Pandey's words are not borrowed wisdom from seminars or theories they are lived experiences carved out of sleepless nights, silent faith, and relentless effort.

What moved me most about this book is its honesty. He doesn't glorify struggle, but he gives it meaning. He doesn't preach success he practices it, and then humbly shows others the path. His story redefines what it means to be a doctor in today's world. It reminds us that true healing begins with healing one's own mindset.

This book arrives at a time when the medical fraternity and indeed all professionals are craving balance between service and self-worth, compassion and confidence, ethics and ambition. Doctor Magnate bridges that gap beautifully. It shows that you can be both grounded and growing, compassionate and courageous, humble and highly successful.

From the narrow bylanes of Maihar to the corridors of leading hospitals, from financial struggle to building a successful hospital and mentoring others Dr. Pandey's journey proves that destiny bows to discipline. His lessons on belief, visualization, gratitude, and consistency are universal. Whether you are a student preparing for NEET, a young doctor starting your practice, or an established professional looking for renewal, this book will speak to your core.

Every page radiates sincerity. Every story carries a lesson. Every quote feels like a conversation with your higher self.

In reading this book, you will not only meet the doctor behind the stethoscope you will meet the human behind the dream. And perhaps, you'll discover a reflection of your own journey, the faith, the fear, the fire.

Dr. Pandey represents a new generation of doctors those who serve with skill, lead with vision, and live with abundance. His life is a message that one can wear the white coat with pride and still build a life of purpose, prosperity, and peace.

May this book inspire every reader to rise above limitations, to walk their own path with integrity, and to believe as Dr. Pandey did that no dream is too distant when your heart beats with conviction.

By Hemsingh Patle, author of the book "The 5-Minute Magical Habits.

FOREWORD

When I first heard about Dr. Anil Pandey, a young boy from a small town in Madhya Pradesh, I wondered what gave him the courage to chase a dream as vast as medicine. But as I got to know his story, I understood: his greatest asset was not opportunity, but unshakable belief

This book, *Doctor Magnate*, is the chronicle of that belief.

It's a story of how grit meets grace, how struggle turns into strength, and how a single dream can transform a life.

Dr. Pandey's narrative captures something rare, the invisible side of success. The discipline of waking up early and the humility to learn from everyone, from teachers to patients. The courage to begin again, even when life said "no." His life stands as living proof that success is not born in comfort, but in conviction.

What sets this book apart is its honesty. It doesn't romanticize hardship, nor does it glorify achievement. It shows the journey in its true essence, the doubt, the faith, the waiting, the breakthroughs. Every page reveals a life lesson. It teaches that no setback is final unless you stop believing.

This book helps us to rise beyond titles and create meaningful impact. It teaches that being a doctor is not only about healing others, but also about healing one's own relationship with purpose and money.

Dr. Pandey's evolution from a student to a surgeon, and from a surgeon to a visionary, reflects the shift every modern professional must make, from survival to significance.

His thoughts on faith, gratitude, and personal growth are not limited to medicine; they transcend disciplines. They remind us that every challenge we face is preparing us for something far greater than what we can currently see.

As you turn these pages, you will not only witness the making of a doctor, you will witness the making of a mindset. One that says:

"You can start anywhere, and still reach everywhere if your heart is honest and your purpose is clear."

May this book inspire you to dream bigger, serve deeper, and live with the same unstoppable faith that has defined Dr. Anil Pandey's journey because the world needs more Doctor Magnates.

Sandeep Singh Tomar,
Managing Director of Savri Personalized & Corporate Gifting

1

Introduction

There was a time when I believed that becoming a doctor was the ultimate dream.

Today, I know—it was only the beginning.

My journey began in the narrow lanes of Maihar, a small town in Madhya Pradesh, known for the divine Sharda Mata Temple, where, as the legend says, the necklace of Mata Sati fell while Lord Shiva carried her burnt body. Like countless others in my town, many parents, students, and even those who had failed before, dreamt of having a doctor in the family.

But I wasn't born into privilege. In those days, I had no access to private tutors or the elite coaching institutes that prepared students for Pre-Medical and Pre-Engineering exams. What I had was sheer perseverance and an unshakable dream. There was no roadmap to success—only a vision stitched into every breath I took: to heal, to serve, to become a doctor.

Behind that dream was hardship. From cleaning crockery shelves to teaching tuitions after school, from walking miles just to afford a book to facing rejection because of money—I lived every chapter of struggle long before I ever held a stethoscope.

And yet, through every hardship, one truth burned brighter than everything else: the fire within me was stronger than the noise around me.

Every night before sleeping, I would close my eyes and visualize myself wearing a white coat. Every morning, I woke up at 4 a.m., repeating silently—

"I will become a doctor."

That single affirmation became my compass through storms of doubt, debt, and disappointment.

When I finally earned my seat at MGM Medical College, Indore, it wasn't just an admission letter—it was proof that faith can outshine fortune.

But life wasn't done teaching me. The white coat didn't just come with prestige; it came with purpose, pain, and pressure. Through the years of medical college—sleepless nights, surgeries, emotional setbacks—I realized something profound: Medicine isn't just about healing others. It's also about healing yourself.

As the years passed, I noticed something deeply unsettling. Brilliant doctors—full of talent, sincerity, and compassion—were struggling, not because they lacked skill, but because they lacked balance.

They served endlessly, yet lived anxiously. They healed others, yet carried invisible wounds within themselves.

That realization became the seed of this book.

Doctor Magnate is not just my story—it's a philosophy. It's about transforming from a doctor of medicine into a doctor of mindset. From being a professional who works hard to survive to a visionary who learns to thrive.

Because medicine is noble—but nobility doesn't mean neglecting your dreams.

Wealth is not a sin. Purpose is not poverty.

When your skills, systems, and spirit align, you create something far greater than a career—you create a legacy.

This book is for every student burning the midnight oil, wondering if the sacrifices are worth it.

For every young doctor drowning in loans, exhaustion, or guilt for wanting a better life.

For every professional who has the skill and the soul, but is missing the strategy.

Through my journey—and the stories of many other Doctor Magnates—you'll discover the habits, mindsets, and practical steps that turn ordinary doctors into extraordinary leaders.

Those who not only save lives but also shape them.

You'll learn how faith turns into focus, how gratitude builds growth, and how discipline births freedom.

You'll also find tender memories of the soft-hearted healers.

And when you finish this book, you won't just feel inspired—you'll feel transformed.

Because this isn't just a story—it's a strategy.

A journey from the stethoscope... to strategy.

Welcome to Doctor Magnate.

From this page onward, you're not just reading a book—you're beginning your transformation.

SECTION 1: STRUGGLE BEHIND THE STETHOSCOPE

This story isn't just mine—it reflects the journey of countless other doctors who rose from humble beginnings, who faced immense pressure, lack of resources, language barriers, and personal pain, yet never gave up. They weren't born with privilege, but with purpose. Gradually in coming chapters we will learn share that how to start our clinical practice and become Doctor magnate.

2

White Coat Dreams, Dusty Beginnings

Childhood, small-town roots, and early sparks of ambition, Faith in self amidst chaos, self-starting without resources.

"Start where you are. Use what you have. Do what you can." — ***Arthur Ash***

"The journey of a thousand miles begins with a single step."— ***Lao Tzu***

"I didn't have much, but I had a dream—and that was enough to start."

Every success story starts somewhere. Mine began in the narrow by-lanes of hardship and uncertainty inside a restless, curious mind—that of a boy in 8th grade, dreaming big while the world around him whispered otherwise. I wasn't born with a silver spoon, nor did I have the privilege of top-tier coaching or a roadmap to follow. It was a pure, innocent dream—sparked not by glamour, but by the urge to heal. But the moment my dream took shape, the world tried to blur it.

Anyone who has ever prepared for a medical entrance exam knows this feeling well — everyone around you tries to scare you. As a biology student, you constantly hear that if you don't get selected in the premedical examination, your life is over and there's no future ahead. And because of this fear, most aspirants lose hope even before they truly begin their preparation — or they study half-heartedly, already defeated by fear rather than failure.

From the very beginning, everyone around me—relatives, neighbors, even some teachers warned us that becoming a doctor required enormous wealth. "How will your family afford it?" they asked. "Only the rich can dream of such things." That we should think "practically." But deep inside, I had already made my decision. I gradually ignored the noise, the opinions, the discouragement—and focused on one thing: study.

Early Experiences: Seeking Light in the Dark

In school, I was an average student, yet something within me burned — a fire to rise above limitations. My family, though loving, couldn't always support the lofty dream of a medical career. Financial struggle was a constant companion, and I often found myself explaining to my heart why some things were not possible — like joining expensive coaching or buying new books.

But sometimes, what you lack in resources, you gain in resilience.

After finishing my 9th-grade exams, I took up a job at a crockery store — not by choice, but by necessity, to support my living and education. Every day, I walked 3 to 4 kilometers to reach the shop. I would open the shutter, clean the glass shelves, doors, racks, tables, and sweep and mop the floor. The crockery there was luxurious — the kind I had never seen before in my life.

Many customers, including some of my own schoolmates, used to visit that store. In the beginning, I felt shy and even embarrassed, working as a cleaning boy while others browsed casually. But over time, the work became routine. The shyness faded.

More importantly, it might not sound like a big deal I learned a priceless lesson: how to handle people, how to stay grounded, and how to focus on my purpose how to stand for hours, and how dignity lies in every form of work, it deepened my understanding of life. I realized that the opinions and voices of others have no power over your work ethic and passion — unless you let them. I realized that no job is small if it brings you closer to your dream.

My brother worked at a nearby medical store, and I often saw doctors visiting there. I didn't even know the difference between a pharmacist and a doctor, and I would ask that pharmacist several times how to become a doctor. He always ignored me. That hurt. But it also made me more curious.

That was the reality of smaller towns—no coaching centers, no mentors, no environment for competitive exams. I didn't even know the differences between homeopathy, allopathy, and Ayurveda. We didn't have seniors to guide us. We were in the dark—but I kept walking.

One day, I met a distant mama at a wedding. He had cracked a medical entrance and was doing BHMS. I asked him how he prepared. He smiled faintly and walked away. Another door closed—but my hunger grew.

The brother of the crockery store owner, a lab technician, once asked me which stream I was choosing after 10th. When I said Biology, he scoffed, "No one from Maihar gets selected in PMT. Don't waste your time—choose Maths. You can start coaching and earn money here." But I didn't listen

Eventually, I left the crockery store to focus more on my studies. To support myself, I started giving tuition classes — primarily in Biology and Math — to students from nearby areas. My journey as a teacher had actually begun much earlier, in Class 8, when I earned INR 30 for tutoring a student from Class 3. I even helped my own batchmates who were struggling with Mathematics.

Teaching not only provided financial relief, but it also shaped me intellectually. Each time I explained a concept to someone else, I understood it more deeply myself. It made me more confident, more articulate. My concepts became sharper — and so did my vision.

In addition to tutoring, I even took part in reading *Kathas* (Hindu spiritual discourses) in the neighborhood. Chanting Sanskrit shlokas during those rituals became a source of both income and inner strength. My voice in worship, powered by devotion and discipline, carried me through some of my toughest days.

My own sister once dreamt of becoming a doctor. She had taken Biology in 11th class, determined to pursue medicine. But under pressure from our uncles, maternal grandparents, and even my mother's sisters, she was forced to switch to Home Science. Her dream was quietly buried—not by failure, but by a lack of support.

Watching her aspirations fade lit a fire in me. Her sacrifice became my silent motivation. Every chapter I studied, every setback I faced, I carried the weight of both our dreams — and I was determined not to let mine be crushed the same way.

Since Vivekanand School had no science stream, I shifted to Government Boys School for Class 11. There, I found something priceless—teachers who believed in me. They reminded me of my potential and did everything they could to help. I didn't even have to pay exam fees in 11th or 12th; Ranjana Shrivastava Ma'am paid for them.

Kavita Ma'am encouraged me to study hard during the entire summer vacation, making me promise on the first day of 12th: "You must top Maihar—and get selected in PMT." That promise ignited a fire within me.

I was blessed to have teachers who believed in me even more than I did at times. During school, some of my teachers recognized my potential and took it upon themselves to ensure I had every possible advantage. They sent me to extra tuition classes, not because I asked, but because they wanted me to prepare more efficiently. What's more touching is—they never charged me a single rupee.

But it wasn't always a phase of pure motivation. During my 11th and 12th, while I was nurturing my dream of becoming a doctor, one of my teachers—who came from the Mathematics stream—once told me:"Intelligent students like you should've taken Maths instead of Biology. In

Maihar, every year, many students go to Kota with dreams of selection. But most return empty-handed and end up doing B.Sc., which doesn't help much in building a career. With Maths, at least you could have gotten into a good government engineering college for a B.E."

His words stung. It wasn't just a comment—it was a seed of doubt, planted by someone I respected. But like always, I refused to listen to external voices. Even then, I believed in the quiet strength of conviction. Even when the world shouted statistics, I followed the whisper of my heart.

"If you hear a voice within you say 'you cannot paint,' then by all means paint, and that voice will be silenced."— ***Vincent Van Gogh***

Looking back now, I realize: it's becoming harder than ever to tune out external noise, especially for young dreamers. To all teachers, mentors, and elders, I have one humble request: Please don't discourage students with negative predictions. Your words carry weight. Use them to lift, not limit. Inspire courage, not confusion. Let the young build their own stories—unshaken by shadows.

I vividly remember attending monthly tests organized by renowned teachers of our town like Ramgopal Dwivedi Sir and Ganesh Agrawal Sir. These tests became my own personal barometer — a way to check where I stood, how much more effort I needed to put in. And gradually, my scores started rising. With every test, my confidence grew stronger. A silent voice within me started whispering, *"Yes, you can top in Maihar. You can even top in MP."*

Then came the board exams. For the Physics paper in 12th, I had left no stone unturned. I wrote every answer with absolute clarity and was sure of a perfect 100 out of 100.But life always has a way of grounding us — gently, but surely.

The same day, after coming home, my Physics teacher, Ganesh Sir, visited. He asked me to walk him through my answers. One by one, I proudly recited them. But when we reached one particular question, I fumbled. My heart sank — I had completely missed it in the exam. It was a small miss, but the impact was deep. That moment taught me something I carry to this day: No matter how well you think you're doing, always stay grounded. Whether it's a grand success or a simple mistake—never lose your patience, and never get overexcited.

I still remember a moment just after my 12th exams when I was given MP PMT exam. A familiar person from our town asked me, "How was your AIPMT exam? You might get selected this year—you were the school topper and even ranked third in Maihar."I looked at him, puzzled. "What is AIPMT?" I asked sincerely. He was surprised. "You don't know? It already happened. The next one will be held after a year."

That moment hit me hard. I had missed one of the most important entrance exams—simply because no one had guided me, no one had informed me. It was a cruel reminder of how far behind we are in smaller towns—not in talent, but in exposure.

Those small moments — a missed question, a free tuition class, a monthly test — they may not seem like milestones. But they shape the mindset of a person preparing for something bigger than himself. They instilled in me a sense of humility, perseverance, and emotional control—the kind that later helped me navigate through even more complex challenges of life.

3

Rocky Road to Kota – Breaking Barriers with Belief

Perseverance despite setbacks, the role of destiny and kindness.

"When you want something, all the universe conspires in helping you to achieve it."— ***Paulo Coelho, The Alchemist***

"Our greatest glory is not in never falling, but in rising every time we fall." — ***Confucius***

One deep longing that lived inside me during my early preparation days was this belief: *"If I could just get the study material from ALLEN, I would definitely get selected."* That thought became so strong, it felt like a key to unlocking my future. I reached out to multiple seniors—those who had taken coaching from Allen. I tried to contact, even requesting personally. But every time, I got the same reply: *"Sorry, I've already passed it on to someone else."*

One of those seniors, a bright girl who eventually got selected that same year and is now a successful obstetrician, had once promised me she would give me her notes. I was filled with hope when she said, *"Come tomorrow morning and collect it.* "That night, I couldn't sleep—thinking about how my fortune was finally changing. But the next morning, when I reached her place, she said casually, *"Oh... I already gave it to my friend."*

That moment crushed me. It felt like my dream of getting into PMT had taken another hit. I was disheartened, disappointed—and honestly, deeply hurt. But looking back now, I realize something magical: Even though I didn't get those notes, my intense desire never left me. That longing was so powerful, it kept me going. I didn't know then, but I understand now: The crux of the book *The Secret* is absolutely true — what you desire with faith and persistence eventually finds its way to you.

I was so determined that I even went to the Chor Bazaar in Jabalpur, hoping I might find second-hand Allen materials there. That's how far I was willing to go. That desire... that fire... it never went out. And maybe that's what really matters—not the material, but the mindset.

You'll read later in this book exactly how The Secret unfolded for me—and how the universe, in its mysterious way, answered my call

After 12th, I was determined to crack the premedical test. But determination alone wasn't enough. I had no strategy, no clear vision, and no real mentorship. I started my preparation from home by buying second-hand MCQ books and referring to whatever little material I could find from seniors.

And in this journey, I must mention a senior who changed the course of my preparation — Rishi Bhaiya. He was the topper of Maihar during his time. Although he didn't pursue a career in medicine, his honesty, clarity, and mentorship were priceless to me. He guided me like an elder brother — what to read, what to avoid, how to think smart.

He handed me a blue-coloured Biology MCQ book, and it became my Geeta. I started solving it with dedication. He also encouraged me to focus on the MP Board textbook MCQs given at the end of each chapter, which later proved to be of great help.

Years later, Rishi Bhaiya carved out his own path. He cleared the Civil Services Exam and is now proudly serving as a Divisional Forest Officer in Jabalpur, Madhya Pradesh. His story and mine — though different in paths — remind me of one thing: If you are hardworking and have a vision, you will reach your destination.

One name that deserves to be written in gold in my life story is Kavita Pandya Ma'am. She was more than just a teacher—she was a believer. While most people saw a boy from a modest background, she saw a future doctor in the making. She left no stone unturned in trying to arrange financial support for my PMT coaching.

She approached big businessmen, local leaders, and even the SDM of Maihar, on my behalf. She was trying everything she could to ensure I wouldn't lose out on a future just because of money.

I still remember...

One respected businessman finally agreed to help and asked me to come to his home. I walked there with a heart full of hope. When I reached, he gave me INR 500. I was thankful—truly I was. But I also knew that coaching fees were at least INR 20,000 at that time in MP. That single note of INR 500 felt both generous and heartbreaking.

Another time, my Biology teacher Atul Garg sir took me all the way to the President of Brahmin Samaj in Satna. He promised to support me—but in the end, I received nothing.

And then, one day, Kavita Ma'am brought me to Dr. Gautam Singh, the SDM of Maihar. He listened to my story, looked at me with respect, and said, *"You're a dedicated student. I'll help."* He asked me to visit his bungalow the next morning. That night, I couldn't sleep. I imagined that this meeting might finally open the door to formal coaching.

The next day, I went with hope. Dr. Singh welcomed me and said, *"You don't need coaching. I'll ask professors from the local college to guide you."* That moment was the final blow to my dream of formal coaching. Not because Dr. Singh didn't want to help—but because there simply was no system in place for students like me. No government scheme, no scholarship, no structure.

Yes, I believed I could study on my own. But I lacked resources. There was no internet, no smartphone, no access to standard books, and I was from a Hindi medium background. I had no clue which book could truly solve my problems. Seeing my struggle, Kavita Ma'am even brought me an English-medium reference book. It was thick... intimidating... and I couldn't even understand the first few pages. That moment broke something inside me. I began to feel like I was losing hope in every direction. But somehow, one little spark of belief—fueled by my teachers, mentors, and a small voice inside me—kept the dream alive.

Whenever I got stuck on Physics and Chemistry problems—and it happened often—I would get frustrated, close the books, and feel overwhelmed. Slowly, laziness took over. I would sleep too much. I didn't know how to self-study efficiently, and coaching felt like a luxury my family couldn't afford. That was when depression began creeping in. The silence of hopelessness started to drown my dream.

But destiny, as always, had other plans.

One day, my school senior Madhav Bhaiya visited our house. After listening to my situation, he explained to my mother that I didn't need full coaching—just Physics and Chemistry classes would be enough. But my mother asked, "Where will he live? Who will provide him food?"

At the same time, my school friend Arvind Gupta's father was planning to send Arvind to Jabalpur for coaching. After discussions, he offered to help me too. He said he would bear the food and rent expenses if my parents could arrange the rest. Somehow, my parents gathered INR 7000—all their savings—and sent me to Jabalpur. We found a small rented room through the sister of my teacher Kavita Pandya Ma'am. Jabalpur was my first turning point.

The Silent Morning That Built a Magnate

From the very first class of my school life, my father used to wake me at 4 a.m. sharp. Day after day, year after year—without a break. At that time, I didn't understand the magic hidden in this ritual. But now, looking back, I know—that simple habit was a game changer. Throughout my student life, this early start became my secret superpower. Today, when I read the book *Miracle Morning* by Hal Elrod, I realize—I was unknowingly following the same practices he describes using the acronym S.A.V.E.R.S.:

- **S – Silence**: I used to pray silently every morning, the moment I opened my eyes.
- **A – Affirmation**: *"Hey Bhagwan, mujhe board exam aur PMT mein achchi rank dila dena."* (Hey God, please help me get a good rank in my board exams and PMT)
- **V – Visualization**: I clearly imagined myself in a white coat, introducing myself as a doctor.
- **E – Exercise**: Walking while reading—on the roads of Maihar, I stayed physically and mentally active.
- **R – Reading**: I read newspapers and real success stories of toppers to stay inspired.
- **S – Scribing**: I noted learnings, formulas, and my deepest thoughts in the margins of my books.

This subconscious ritual gave me strength, even when my environment tried to break me.

Discipline Over Distractions

During my student life, I hardly remember attending any distant relative's marriage. Not because I didn't care, but because I was fiercely protecting my time and focus. Maybe at that time they didn't understand me—or even criticized me—but I was driven by a dream. If you're dreaming big, you must limit all those activities that don't serve your growth. I'm not saying don't be social—but choose your presence wisely. Once you reach your optimal position, the same people who missed you at events will praise your success and forget your absence.

If you think you can watch movies, attend all weddings, be present everywhere, and still crack a tough competitive exam—you're lying to yourself. This is the very reason why only a few achieve top ranks, while others have to compromise on their dreams or their stream. Success demands focus, not just effort.

Setbacks, Sacrifices, and Survival

To chase my medical dream, I moved to Jabalpur and joined Momentum Coaching. There, I built a routine that would test the limits of my discipline — waking up at 3 a.m., studying relentlessly until midnight. That hard work soon began to show results. Out of a class of 50 students, I consistently secured 3rd or 4th rank. It wasn't just about marks — it was about proving to myself that I *belonged* in this race.

My journey in Jabalpur was anything but smooth. I stayed with Arvind, and we managed everything on our own — cooking, cleaning, and surviving without any tiffin service or luxury. Life was tough, but I had accepted it. However, Arvind often turned off his alarm and later blamed me for waking up late. Things got worse when he complained to *Ma'am's sister*, who ended up scolding me without knowing the full truth.

Eventually, Arvind left — and I was left alone to bear the full rent. That's when I was asked to shift into a tiny room that had earlier been used for their dog. That moment... was deeply painful. But I didn't complain. I quietly accepted it. Because somewhere inside, I believed that enduring silently today would shape a stronger version of me tomorrow.

The Hands That Lifted Me

There was a time in my life when I had nothing—no money, no resources, and barely any emotional strength left. Yet, each day, I gathered whatever courage I had and approached someone—anyone—hoping for a little support, a word of guidance, or just a listening ear.

That difficult phase taught me something invaluable: the true power of human connection. What people today call networking, I experienced in its rawest form—as an act of survival, not strategy. That lesson has stayed with me to this day, helping me not just emotionally, but professionally.

One act of kindness from that time still shines like a light in my memory. Mr. Narayan Tripathi, who was an MLA then, visited my father's pan shop one day. Without us even asking, he quietly handed over INR 5,000. That money wasn't just cash—it was hope. It meant food, a few more days of coaching, another step toward the dream.

And he wasn't the only one. Throughout my journey, many great souls helped me silently, selflessly, without expecting anything in return. I have never forgotten their kindness. And because of them, I never allowed myself to lose hope completely.

Help came again when Sunil Mishra offered me a place to stay during my preparation days. I shifted there with gratitude in my heart, hoping for stability. But soon, my performance began to dip. The distractions around me, the lack of personal space, and emotional restlessness began affecting my focus. My ranks fell, and so did my confidence.

Eventually, it became impossible for my parents to continue paying my fees. I was forced to leave coaching. Heartbroken, I returned to Maihar—mentally shattered, emotionally drained, and spiritually lost. I tried to continue my self-study, but nothing seemed to work. That phase felt like being trapped in a dark tunnel with no end in sight. For the first time, hopelessness felt permanent.

The Greatest Lesson

One of the most important lessons I learned is this: Never feel ashamed or hesitant in doing anything that adds value to your growth, your career, or your character. If it builds you, it's worth it. Even if it means asking for help, even if it means being misunderstood, even if it means staying away from distractions.

"Your network is your net worth." – ***Porter Gale***

"Ask, and it will be given to you; seek, and you will find." – ***Matthew 7:7***

These were the building blocks of my resilience, and the foundation of my journey to becoming a Doctor Magnate.

There's a memory that still sends a chill down my spine. Back then, I always traveled in general coaches. Overcrowded, noisy, suffocating.

I'd often enter with one foot still in the air, squeezing into a space that barely existed.

But one journey stands out. In the middle of that suffocating chaos, I closed my eyes and began to imagine. I saw myself sitting in a comfortable AC coach. People around me were asking about my career and future. And I, with quiet pride, answered: "I'm pursuing MBBS." That moment—though entirely imagined—felt real. I lived that dream in my mind long before it came true in reality.

Back then, I didn't even know about books like *The Power of Your Subconscious Mind* by Joseph Murphy. I had never heard of *The Secret* or the law of attraction. But now, after reading these books, I realize—That was my subconscious mind manifesting my destiny. That one mental image kept me moving through the toughest days. And today, I tell every student, every young dreamer: Imagine big. Feel it. Live it—even before it happens. Your mind doesn't know the difference between imagination and reality.

Your dreams may seem miles away, but they're just one clear vision away from becoming your reality. I gave the PMT exam and scored 79%, but I was not selected.

"Believe you can and you're halfway there." — **Theodore Roosevelt**

I thought it was over. But God had one more plan—this time, in the form of Sunil Mishra's father, who suggested Allen, Kota. Kota was a dream for serious aspirants, but its fee—INR 40,000—was unreachable. Sunil's father promised to bear my living expenses, but not the tuition fee. Miraculously, our land had been sold, and the money kept for my sister's marriage was still lying unused. My parents gave me INR 20,000, and I left for Kota.

I requested the Director at Allen to allow me to pay the fees in two installments — and to my relief, they agreed. After just seven days of classes, I appeared for my first test and secured a rank above 500 out of 2,500 students. That one result filled me with newfound confidence. But just as I began to believe in myself, reality hit me hard.

One morning, I was stopped at the coaching gate. The guard took my ID and directed me to the accounts office. There, I was told plainly: *"Deposit the pending fees, or you can't attend any more classes."* At that moment, everything came crashing down.

The old picture of Jabalpur flashed before my eyes — the pain of being forced to leave coaching because I couldn't afford the remaining fees and returned back to Maihar. And now, it was happening all over again. This time, it felt even worse. I was doing well, I had momentum, I had belief... and yet, I was being pulled back by something beyond my control.

I was devastated. It felt like the dream of becoming a doctor was slipping away — not because of lack of ability, but because of financial constraints. The sadness... the regret... the helplessness of a weaker financial background cut deep into my spirit. For a moment, I truly felt like giving up.

In desperation, I went to meet Director Brajesh Maheshwari Sir. He looked through my academic background and said firmly: *"With 91%, in higher secondary there's no guarantee of selection. If your rank is 500 and you're from a Hindi-medium background, it's going to be very hard to make it. So please — deposit the remaining fees or leave. We'll provide you with the study material, but you won't be allowed to attend classes."*

His words hit me like a wall. I started calling and messaging friends — begging them for help. Everyone politely declined. Sunil Mishra's father had already helped once — I couldn't ask again. That evening, I sat down and packed my bag silently, tears rolling down my cheeks. There was no drama, no outburst — just a quiet surrender. I had fought so hard, but now it seemed like I had no choice. I was ready to return to Maihar, not because I gave up on my dream — but because I had run out of ways to hold on to it.

Before leaving, I went to see my second test result: I had secured 33rd rank out of 2500. That rank changed everything. I ran to Brajesh Sir.

He hadn't seen the result yet. His assistant confirmed my rank. Immediately, Sir asked me to stay. He waived off most of the remaining fees and said: "Deposit only INR 3000 when you can. Just maintain this rank." I stayed. I worked harder than ever.

The Power of Understanding

In Kota, for the first time in my life, I felt what it truly meant to study with full concentration. I attended every single class without fail—and not just physically, but mentally present, completely immersed. My focus never wavered. The faculty there weren't just subject experts—they were humble, compassionate, and student-friendly.

They had a rare gift: they could take even the toughest topics and break them down into simple, digestible parts. And for someone like me, from a Hindi-medium background, that made all the difference. For the first time, I felt truly seen, understood, and empowered.

I began to believe in myself with a conviction I'd never felt before. And I can proudly say—"Yes, I understood everything. And yes, I *will* get selected." My routine was a warrior's routine: Wake up at 4:00 AM, Study till 10:00 PM, 6 hours of coaching classes

No holidays. No distractions. Just one mission.

There were no parties, no outings, no TV shows, no mobile. But there was consistency, and that was enough. Discipline became my best friend. And for the first time, I truly started believing that I was on the right path.

When I first arrived in Kota, I stayed with Sunil Mishra—a friendly and supportive boy from a well-to-do family. We both came with dreams, but our paths soon diverged. While I walked 5 to 6 kilometers daily to attend coaching classes with full dedication, Sunil, despite his good nature, rarely went. He had a decent mobile phone and spent much of his time talking to friends and enjoying the comforts his father provided.

Over time, his friends began frequenting our room, turning it into a hub of distractions. I observed a sharp contrast forming—while one of us was relentlessly focused, the other was sliding into a comfort zone, shielded by financial privilege but unaware of its dangerous lull.

This experience taught me something profound: parental love should empower, not spoil. Facilities, if not balanced with discipline, can become the enemy of growth. I began to believe strongly that being pushed by circumstances makes you stronger, while being pampered can make you weak.

Eventually, the distractions became unbearable. I made the difficult decision to move out and live alone to protect my focus. But then came another blow—my parents were no longer able to send money for rent or food. I visited multiple places searching for a minimal room, sometimes skipping meals, sometimes holding back tears during a bath, just to hide my pain from the world.

Fire in the Belly

Life in Kota wasn't just about lectures and libraries. It was also about learning to survive—with dignity, with silence, and with unmatched willpower. There was a small, almost invisible ritual I followed—one that still humbles me when I remember it. Every Sunday evening, the mess would be closed. No dinner. No backup.

While many students would go out for food, I had no such luxury. Instead, I would quietly walk to a nearby shop and buy one small packet of Parle-G biscuits. Back in my room, I'd take my steel glass, fill it with plain drinking water—and slowly dip each biscuit in the water, softening it so it wouldn't feel too dry in my mouth.

But believe me—there was no sadness in it. In fact, in those moments, I felt an odd sense of pride... a strange joy. Because I knew:"This hunger is part of my journey. One day, I'll tell this story not with shame—but with strength." *"Success is sweet. The sweeter when it's earned with sacrifice."*

During one such emotional moment, I remembered my sister—she had left our family years ago under painful circumstances related to societal pressures around marriage and dowry. I missed her deeply tears were in my eyes, thinking how things might have been different if society had allowed us to treat daughters as equals, as friends.

But then, something miraculous happened. One day, while I was sitting in the room, Sunil Mishra's mobile rang. It was my long-lost sister. She had somehow reconnected with us—through the very friend whose distractions had led me to this low point. She told me not to worry about money anymore.

Every month, she started sending me enough to cover my rent and food. She even sent me a small Micromax mobile phone so I could stay connected. I still remember that ringtone like a heartbeat of hope. If my sister hadn't re-entered my life at that moment, I might never have become a doctor.

This phase taught me the essence of inner strength, divine timing, and how faith and family—even in their unexpected forms—can be life-changing. It taught me that pain is not your enemy; it is your sculptor. And most importantly, it taught me that when you pursue your dream with sincerity, the universe will conspire to help you.

As time passed in Kota, I began to see the results of my dedication. Consistently, I started ranking under 50 in regular tests. There was a moment I'll never forget—Director Brajesh Maheshwari Sir once said during our regular session: "If I ever call any student 'Doctor' from this stage, he or she will definitely become a doctor."

That sentence hit me like a blessing. It became my affirmation. After every test, we had open sessions—our teachers would encourage us, celebrate our improvements, and distribute medals to the top 20 rankers. With time, I became one of them. That medal around my neck wasn't just a piece of metal; it was a promise of what was to come.

I made the library my second home. Even as many students began leaving Kota due to burnout or emotional exhaustion, I stayed till the very end—holding on with sheer grit. This is the time when most students drift, but if you can push through the fatigue and loneliness at the end, the dream is already half won.

In my final days there, I stayed with another determined student—Hemant. We had an unspoken pact: to help each other wake up early and not miss a single study hour. In that companionship, I found strength and accountability.

I appeared for the AIPMT Pre-exam and cleared it. But the journey didn't end there. I had to travel to Jaipur for the Mains exam. With no one accompanying me, I boarded a crowded train alone, holding on to faith more than anything else. Upon reaching Jaipur, I didn't inform my sister or my parents—I didn't want to burden them.

I went in search of the lowest budget hotel, but most were fully booked. Finally, I requested a hotel manager to allow me a spot just to sleep. He was kind enough to let me rest in the waiting area for the night. That's where I spent the night—on a bench, under dim lights, wrapped in dreams of making it.

The next morning, I appeared for the Mains exam. I felt a slight pang of regret as I realized I hadn't practiced written question formats properly during the year. I gave it my best but knew it wasn't my strongest performance.

Later, I also cracked BHU Pre, but couldn't clear its Mains. Yet I never gave up. Every setback only reinforced my resolve. Every difficulty sharpened my focus. Because becoming a doctor isn't just about knowledge—it's about endurance, sacrifice, and unwavering belief in your own journey.

4

Dream Manifested - Faith, Struggle & Serendipity

Power of belief, miracles born out of persistence and subconscious desire.

"*Whatever the mind can conceive and believe, it can achieve."— **Napoleon Hill***

"Faith is taking the first step even when you don't see the whole staircase." — ***Martin Luther King Jr.***

The Turning Point – Destiny Doesn't Miss the Deserving

After months of relentless preparation, I finally reached the day of the MPPMT exam, held in Satna. The morning session went smoothly—I was calm, focused, and deeply immersed in the paper. During the break between the two sessions, my mentor, P.N. Sharma Sir, called me and asked gently: "How was the paper?" I smiled, confident and composed, and replied: "Sir, I will definitely get selected."

That wasn't just optimism—it was conviction. A belief born from sacrifice, unwavering consistency, and years of silent faith. That evening, as I returned to Maihar, I was still carrying the energy of the exam, replaying questions in my mind, visualizing results. Just then—my phone rang. It was Sharma Sir again. His tone was calm, but serious. "Beta," he said, *"main bas yeh poochhne ke liye call kar raha hoon—AIPMT ka result aa gaya hai. Check kiya kya?"* (I called mainly to ask this — the AIPMT result is out. Have you checked it?)

He called me and asked me, softly yet directly, if I had seen the result. My heart began to race. My palms turned cold. I didn't speak—I just asked him my result. There was a pause on the other end. He tried to soften the blow. *"Tension mat le... tum MPPMT mein definitely select ho jaoge."* (Don't take tension... you will definitely get selected in MPPMT).

But I could sense it. He was hiding something. Eventually, he told me. Rank: Around 6000. It wasn't enough. In that moment, everything froze. I had just declared to my mentor, with unwavering faith, that I'd make it. And now this? Doubt. Disappointment. Silence.

But then—within that silence—something shifted. I whispered to myself, "No, this isn't the end. This is just one door closing. MPPMT is still there. My dream isn't broken." I refused to let that rank define me. Instead, I used it as fire. That call from Sharma Sir wasn't just about a result. It was a turning point—a quiet whisper from the universe that true faith is tested not in success, but in how we handle setbacks.

And just a few days later, destiny would prove why the one who doesn't quit... always finds the way. God never abandons dreamers. He just tests them a little longer.

"The only limit to our realization of tomorrow is our doubts of today."— ***Franklin D. Roosevelt***

And then, the MPPMT results were declared. Rank: 155. All over Madhya Pradesh. I had done it. I was selected. The power of the subconscious mind is real. My heart always longed for something greater—even when doubt clouded my thoughts. When I got 155th rank in MPPMT, I wasn't entirely sure whether I'd get an MBBS seat.

That morning, I was browsing the newspaper and saw the name of Nitin Pandey, one of my Allen coaching mates, in the selected list. That made me jump with excitement—and also triggered the anxiety of waiting for my own result.

I met my schoolmate Anurag's elder brother, who was a BHMS doctor. He told me I might get BDS only or MBBS from Rewa. That gave me hope. I had secured 89.9%, and deep inside, I held a strong faith in God and myself—I wanted only one thing: a seat in MGM Medical College, Indore. I still remember Neetu Singh Ma'am, my Hindi teacher, confidently telling me one day: "You'll definitely get Indore."

When the time for counselling came, we had no money. We borrowed INR 10,000 from my Bijju Mama to appear for counseling. As I entered the counselling room, only two unreserved MBBS seats were left in Indore. One was reserved for a female candidate. My heart sank. But then, destiny intervened. The candidate ranked above me chose Gwalior, not Indore. I couldn't believe it—the last general seat at MGM Medical College, Indore, was mine.

WOW. It felt magical. A miracle. I had earned a seat at MGM Medical College, Indore—one of the top medical colleges in the state. The impossible... had just become my reality.

I remembered the sleepless nights. The walking miles. The pain of being broke, being alone, and still pushing forward. I remembered Sunil, the library, the medals, the missed meals—and the unwavering belief.

*"Success is not final, failure is not fatal: It is the courage to continue that counts."— **Winston Churchill***

That day, it wasn't just a result. It was proof that faith, effort, and resilience always win—eventually. But the struggle was far from over.

There was no land left with my parents to use as collateral, and no bank was ready to give an education loan. I applied at SBI, but the bank manager, Mr. Tiwari, whose own daughter was doing MBBS in Jabalpur, declined it. The last date for fee submission was 31st July 2008. Days passed. I felt helpless.

On 29th July, I met Motilal Tiwari Ji, MLA of that time. He called the SBI manager personally and requested him to approve the loan. And by 4 pm the same day—we had the INR 40,000 demand draft in our hands. It was nothing short of divine intervention.

There's one more thing I must share...In every entrance exam—AIPMT, MPPMT, AIIMS, AFMC, and BHU—I always travelled alone, in general coach, without any fear. Most other students came with parents or siblings, but I didn't have that privilege. Yet, I learned how to stay strong, focused, and independent. This is a message to today's youth: you don't need luxury or constant support—you need courage and clarity.

After securing my seat, I stayed at a relative's house in Indore. My seniors advised me to avoid the college hostel due to rampant ragging. That's when I connected with Dr. Gautam Singh, who was an SDM in Maihar during my school years and had recently been transferred to Indore. He helped me get a private hostel, though it was far from medical college. I used to travel by bus daily.

After 2–3 months, some of my batchmates—Nitin, Abhishek, and Vijay—offered me to share their flat at a minimal rent. That was a turning point in my college life. Over time, I lived with the same group—my batchmates and seniors—throughout my MBBS journey. For the first time in a long time, I felt a sense of belonging. These friendships became my emotional anchor.

5

Survival to Self-Discovery - My Early MBBS Days

In the beginning, I was just trying to survive MBBS — but somewhere along the way, I discovered who I really was.

"Life isn't about finding yourself. Life is about creating yourself."— ***George Bernard Shaw***

"In the middle of difficulty lies opportunity." — ***Albert Einstein***

Entering MGM Medical College, Indore was a dream realized — a combination of grit, grace, and miracles. But the dream was just the beginning. I soon discovered that surviving MBBS wasn't just about textbooks or tests. It was about learning life at a whole new level.

The academic pressure during MBBS was intense. Most of the students around me came from English-medium backgrounds—confident, well-prepared, and quick in making their own notes.I, on the other hand, came from a modest Hindi-medium background. Just to keep pace, I often had to study each chapter multiple times.

I translated difficult terms line by line, asked doubts without hesitation—no matter how basic they seemed—and stayed up late night after night, determined not to fall behind. It wasn't easy, but I had made up my mind: I might take longer, but I will not give up.

"It does not matter how slowly you go as long as you do not stop."— ***Confucius***

During practicals and ward postings, I often felt like an outsider—awkward, unsure, and out of place. But deep inside, something had shifted. I was no longer afraid of the struggle. Instead, I had learned to embrace my weaknesses and work on them with quiet determination.

In the initial months, I faced humiliation—for my poor English, my modest dressing, and sometimes even for my hesitation during patient interactions. But I didn't let that break me. I used that discomfort as fuel for self-improvement.

I started improving my spoken English, carefully observed how toppers studied, learned how to make smart notes, strategized for university exams, and practiced how to present cases confidently during clinical rounds. Every small step was part of a bigger transformation—from insecurity to inner strength.

Money was still a constraint. I couldn't afford all textbooks, so I borrowed, photocopied, or bought used ones. I ate frugally and skipped social outings. But I had a goal, and everything else was secondary.

"Discipline is the bridge between goals and accomplishment."— ***Jim Rohn***

Slowly, things started changing. I began performing better in internal exams. Teachers started noticing me. My confidence grew. I started believing I didn't just "get lucky" — I belonged here. And I was ready to prove it.

"Hardships often prepare ordinary people for an extraordinary destiny."— ***C.S. Lewis***

The seniors welcomed me with a lesson: "Don't just study. Enjoy this journey. These are the golden years you'll remember forever." And they were right. The first six months of college were filled with what we called "introduction sessions"—more famously known as ragging.

At the time, it felt strange, even difficult. We had to memorize the names of all seniors and our batchmates. We had to use only the "third button" of our shirts, walk without eye contact, and follow quirky, sometimes humiliating instructions. We were shouted at, asked to do bizarre things—sometimes removing most of our clothes, sometimes abusing our friends just to entertain the seniors.

But slowly, we realized—it was a ritual of bonding. After every ragging session, the same seniors would take us to restaurants, feed us the best food, and pay the bill. They became our mentors, protectors, and even our family. There was an unspoken rule: "If any senior is around when we're at a tea stall or snack shop, they'll pay the bill—no matter how much we order.

They gave us bone sets, books, notes, and most importantly—guidance. They taught us not just how to study, but how to carry ourselves as doctors—how to dress, talk, and maintain respect and dignity in every interaction.

It wasn't easy, but it was real. That's how we grew. Together. Through shared food, laughter, late-night study sessions, surprise viva scares, heartbreaks, and endless cups of tea—our batch became more than classmates. We were brothers and sisters in struggle. Each one of us had a story worth telling. And this chapter of life? It taught me one thing clearly: When you walk alone, you might walk fast. But when you walk together—you walk far.

Bonds Beyond Batches

"A mentor is not someone who walks ahead of you to show you how they did it. A mentor walks alongside you to show you what you can become."— ***Unknown***

The bonding with seniors during my early MBBS days was one of the most beautiful and impactful aspects of my medical journey. Even today, I am in close touch with seniors who were five or more years ahead of me—many of whom have become renowned names in the medical world. They are now working in top hospitals, have built strong reputations, and established themselves like tycoons in their respective specialties.

What sets them apart, however, is not just their success—it's their humility and unwavering support. I'm grateful to mentors like Dr. Krishna Sir, Dr. Lalan Sir, Dr. Mukesh Sir, and many more, who have always been just a phone call away. Whether it's help with a complex patient case, guidance on a tough decision, or simply words of encouragement, they have never hesitated to stand by me. Their support continues even today, and they are among the real heroes who inspired me to write this book.

Back then, ragging—although intense—often transformed into mentorship. What began as a tough introduction to college life evolved into deep mutual respect, strong friendships, and lifelong guidance. While I strongly support the strict prohibition of ragging today (as no form of harassment is acceptable), I also feel that something valuable has been lost in the process: meaningful senior-junior bonding.

Today, I barely know juniors from even two or three batches below me. That regular interaction, that sense of being part of one large family, seems to have faded. And yet, in our profession, that very network is golden. We still use those old connections—whether for referrals, second opinions, job opportunities, or moral support. It's a huge, often underrated strength in our field.

I believe we need to revive that spirit of connection—not through force, but through mentorship. Through structured, respectful, and voluntary interactions. Because beyond academics and surgeries, medicine is about people. And a single word of encouragement from a senior at the right moment can transform a life.

Turning Pain into Purpose

One evening, on 10th August 2010, while returning from a tuition class — I was teaching Biology to the daughter of a judge — I was riding my batchmate Pushpraj's Hero Hunk motorcycle. Around 6 PM, near the busy streets of Indore, I collided with an Activa rider who turned out to be the brother of an Orthopaedic surgeon. The accident was devastating.

I had suffered a bimalleolar fracture in my ankle joint — my foot was literally hanging like a limp ball. Despite the excruciating pain, I immediately called my friend Abhash, and nearby locals helped me reach a nearby hospital. There, I received first aid: painkillers and a below-knee slab.

Fate intervened when Dr. Sanjay Awasiya, a chest physician who often visited that hospital, heard that an MGM medical student was admitted. He came to see me, and without hesitation, contacted Dr. Sunil Rajan, one of the most respected Orthopaedic surgeons in the city. I was shifted to MY Hospital, and admitted under his care.

After accident, we mutually agreed not to file one, which I later realized could have been risky.

When Dr. Sunil Rajan Sir visited me, he simply smiled and said, "*Badhiya ho jayega tu.*" (You'll recover soon) These words were so simple, yet powerful — they held the assurance and comfort that only a great doctor could offer.

That period of pain and stress also made me proud to have such warm-hearted batchmates and seniors. My room was always full of them—they made me laugh, brought me different recipes to try, constantly motivated me, and thanks to them, even when I underwent surgery, I never felt the weight of time passing. The day of my discharge felt almost forgotten.

Coincidentally, 15th August 2010 was the day of JUDA strike (Junior Doctors' Association). Still, I was the only patient operated on that day. It felt nothing short of a miracle. My elder brother came and stayed with me day and night. We didn't inform our parents until after the surgery. He protected me like a shield, and I could feel his worry masked behind his calm.

That incident — the pain, the vulnerability, the treatment, the care, and the healing — changed my life forever. From that day, I decided, "I will become an Orthopaedic Surgeon." It wasn't a career choice anymore. It was a calling.

6

Failing Forward

Facing failure, bouncing back, and the mindset shift

*"It is not in the stars to hold our destiny but in ourselves." – **William Shakespeare***

*"I have not failed. I've just found 10,000 ways that won't work."— **Thomas Edison***

The transformation from a student into a doctor doesn't happen the day you receive your degree—it's a slow evolution, built through countless small decisions, silent sacrifices, and moments of quiet strength. My journey through the final year and internship was filled with both inspiration and interruptions, focus and frustration, but above all—a relentless pursuit of growth.

The Aftermath of the Accident

After my ankle surgery, the road to recovery was not just about healing physically—it tested me emotionally and mentally. The bike involved in the accident had been seized by the police, and I had to make repeated visits to the police station and court to sort things out. All of this, while I was confined to a below-knee slab, moving around with the support of a walker—and this time, without any family member by my side.

Eventually, I even had to go to court to secure bail for the bike. During this difficult time, Dr. Sanjay Awasiya Sir and Dr. Arvind Shukla Sir stood by me like guardians. Thanks to their unwavering support and efforts, the issue was finally resolved through a mutual agreement.

That challenging episode taught me a crucial life lesson: never take legal precautions lightly. No matter how familiar the person involved is—even if they're from a medical background—always insist on filing an MLC (Medico-Legal Case). In moments of crisis, emotions should never override legal wisdom.

The Comeback: Discipline & Determination

Life has a unique way of testing us—not just physically, but mentally and emotionally. One of the most difficult phases in my MBBS journey came when I suffered an ankle fracture. I had already committed myself to working hard starting from my second professional year, but the injury hit me at a crucial moment. I was bedridden and missed nearly 2 to 3 months of classes. The syllabus kept piling up, and the burden soon began to crush my confidence.

As I watched my classmates move forward, I felt stuck—falling deeper into self-doubt. I began slipping into a silent depression. Everything I had planned seemed to be falling apart. It felt like I was losing the battle even before truly entering the war. At that low point, I was left with only two choices:

Either I could sit with my regrets and stay trapped in that darkness, or I could gather the broken pieces of my spirit and push myself forward. Gradually my confidence started coming back. Slowly but surely, I found my rhythm again.

Once I recovered physically, I returned with renewed energy and intensity. I had no time to waste. Every morning at 7 AM, I would head straight to the reading room—fondly called the "box"—where we MBBS students buried our heads in books from sunrise till midnight. The pain, the hospital visits, the police formalities—all the suffering—had done something remarkable: it sharpened my focus.

That phase taught me two powerful lessons: Sometimes, pain becomes your greatest fuel. And sometimes, you are the only person who can believe in yourself enough to help you rise again.

Final Year: Seeds of Excellence

By this time, my goals were becoming clearer. I was leaning strongly toward orthopaedics, inspired by my own injury and the brilliant work of Dr. Sunil Rajan Sir. The final year was intense, with massive subjects like medicine, surgery, paediatrics, and more. But I found myself enjoying the grind. I still continued tuition classes—financially it was essential, but more than that, it kept me mentally sharp and socially grounded.

Internship: Sharpening the Sword

Internship was where the real test began. It wasn't just about books anymore—it was about action, responsibility, and emotional resilience. I still remember first time when I puncture the vein of patient in obstetrics and gynaecology ward for giving IV fluids I was nervous. The adrenaline rush of managing patients, counselling anxious relatives, and making real-time decisions taught me more in a day than weeks in a classroom.

During this phase, I formed a strong study circle with Chandu and Arun. The three of us pushed each other every single day—discussing clinical cases, previous year PG questions, and building strategies for the NEET PG exam. We regularly aced the Bhatia Test Series, which became our confidence booster. It truly felt like our selection was within reach.

Unlike other fields where you move forward after graduation, in medicine, the competition doesn't end—it only intensifies. Every student must pass through the fiery gates of the Pre-PG entrance, and that requires clarity, planning, and discipline.

One harsh truth I observed is that many students lose direction once they secure an MBBS seat. They feel the destination has been reached—but that's far from reality. MBBS is not the final goal; it's just the foundation. That's where balance becomes crucial. You can enjoy your newfound adulthood, but without a clear path ahead, it's easy to drift. Today, I can clearly see the consequences.

Batchmates who hadn't decided their goal early on struggled—not just in academics but in life decisions too. Some spent 3 to 5 years figuring out their branch or trying to crack the exam again. Some, unfortunately, lost the thread entirely and even failed their first year.

And in medical colleges, failing the first year can be isolating. You get detached from your original batch—socially and academically—and that hits hard. I've seen talented people lose confidence just because of that disconnect. Thankfully, I stayed focused. I had a clear vision: Orthopaedics. That clarity helped me sail through internship with discipline and energy. I studied intensely, fueled by purpose, not pressure.

"The only thing worse than being blind is having sight but no vision"— ***Helen Keller***

"You will never always be motivated, so you must learn to be disciplined"— ***Unknown***

An Unexpected Setback

Just two to three months into my internship—when I was at the peak of my performance and test results—a sudden jolt shook my world. My mother slipped and sustained an olecranon fracture. Coincidentally, she was admitted and operated on in the same hospital where I was working. Seeing her as a patient, lying on a stretcher in the corridors I used to walk with confidence, was emotionally overwhelming.

But despite the pain and distraction, I didn't let it derail my focus or preparation. I compartmentalized my emotions, learned to stay composed under pressure, and kept moving forward. That incident became another reminder: in medicine—and in life—resilience isn't optional; it's essential.

My Mother – My First Hero

My mother is one of the strongest people I have ever seen in my life. Even after suffering a fracture, she never became overly emotional, sentimental, or tearful. Her strength was in her calm—she remained positive, composed, and resilient through it all.

She never pressured me to choose a particular stream or career path. Instead, she simply motivated me with unwavering faith, always saying, *"You will definitely get selected."* That quiet confidence she had in me became my backbone.

What still amazes me is how quickly she resumed her work after the fracture—never once making me feel burdened or responsible. Because of her strength and sacrifice, I was able to focus even harder on my studies, knowing that someone was silently holding everything together behind the scenes. She was—and always will be—the real hero of my life.

I continued studying, giving my best, and sat for NEET PG. Unfortunately, I scored a rank of around 6000. Deep down, I knew this wouldn't get me a seat in Orthopaedics. It was disappointing, but not devastating. Because one thing had become clear—I had no plans of giving up. So, I stood up again. I took a deep breath, gathered my strength, and started preparing for the next attempt.

"The world breaks everyone, and afterward, some are strong at the broken places."— ***Ernest Hemingway***

7

The Silent Anchor

"Still waters run deep."- ***Unknown***

"Some people arrive and make such a beautiful impact on your life, you can barely remember what life was like without them." – ***Anna Taylor***

In the noise of medical college life, her quiet presence became my calm—she didn't speak much, but her silent support held me steady when everything else felt uncertain.

In the chaotic rhythm of my MBBS journey—where sleepless nights, exam stress, and medical dreams occupied every inch of my mind—there existed a quiet, tender memory that never left me.

She lived with her family in the same apartment complex where I stayed. Always respectful and soft-spoken, she would greet me with a smile and call me "Sir," as I was her immediate senior.

We shared casual conversations—mostly about studies. I often guided her on what topics to focus on or how to prepare. Though I always kept my boundaries clear, there was something unspoken between us—a calm admiration, a silent warmth.

The Ride That Shook Me

At that time, I didn't have my own vehicle. Every day, I walked to college—focused, detached, and fully immersed in my thoughts. I remember often thinking about her. She was always so pretty, always smiling.

One morning, as I walked, I didn't know why, but my mind kept drifting to her. Suddenly, a Scooty Pep pulled up beside me. The rider had her face covered with a scarf.

"Sir, will you come? I'll drop you to college," she offered.

I was caught off guard, and before I could respond, she removed the scarf. It felt surreal, like an illusion. I hesitated for a moment, unsure whether to accept. But in the end, I climbed on.

The short ride changed something in me. For a few seconds, my heartbeat raced, my body went cold with surprise—not because anything extraordinary happened, but because for the first time in a while, I felt... seen. Cared for. I wasn't alone anymore.

But the relief was short-lived. As soon as I arrived at college, I found myself unable to focus. My mind kept wandering back to that ride, to her voice, her gesture. I couldn't get it out of my head.

That evening, after some deep reflection, I decided to act. I messaged her:

"Please don't offer me a lift again."

It wasn't easy. I knew it might hurt her. But I had made a promise to myself—to stay disciplined, no matter the distraction. My goal was clear, and I couldn't afford to let anything, not even the kindest of gestures, pull me off course.

A Silent Source of Strength

She respected my decision. She never brought it up. She didn't need to. In that quiet understanding, I found something far more meaningful than a conversation: a deep, unspoken respect.

It wasn't that I had no space in my life for love or affection—I had simply made a promise to myself. The focus on my goals was non-negotiable.

Was she someone I dated? Was she a typical love story? She was, however, something far more profound—a spark of purity, a beacon of genuine human connection.

Even today, when I look back at those days, without remembering her, my story of inspiration feels incomplete. Her presence, though silent, was the quiet strength that reminded me that being focused doesn't mean being heartless. Sometimes, the most unexpected forms of love and inspiration come from the least likely sources.

Her quiet support was never about grand gestures or romantic overtures. It was about the steadiness of her presence, the gentleness in her words, and the warmth in her eyes that made me feel seen—not as a student or a doctor-to-be, but as a person who was simply doing his best.

The Final Chapter of That Chapter

While I had given my all—every ounce of hard work and discipline—for preparing for the NEET-PG exam, she was just starting her internship and preparing with equal determination. She used to attend coaching classes and, in the evenings, she would sit with me and explain difficult topics patiently.

Whatever gaps I had left in my preparation the previous year, she helped me fill them. She motivated me constantly to keep reading, to stay focused, and to believe that my dream branch was within reach.

Finally, the day came—I got selected and secured my MS Orthopaedics seat. But destiny had its own plan. She didn't make it that year.

The happiness of my success suddenly felt incomplete. She cried. I was silent. Somewhere deep inside, I wished the story had ended differently.

But life, as always, teaches you balance—joy and pain, victory and loss, all woven together in a single thread of destiny.

In this book, somewhere between the lines, you may find a glimpse of her. And in the second part of this book, you may come to know what destiny had written for our story—was it complete, or beautifully unfinished? Because some people don't stay to be a part of your future—they come to shape it, and then quietly disappear, leaving behind strength, gratitude, and silence.

Some anchors don't make noise.
They just hold you steady—
Until you're strong enough to stand on your own.

8

The Orthopaedics Odyssey

My Orthopaedics Journey Begins

*"The gem cannot be polished without friction, nor man perfected without trials." – **Chinese Proverb***

*"Hardships often prepare ordinary people for an extraordinary destiny." – **C.S. Lewis***

Orthopaedics didn't welcome me with open arms—it threw me straight into the fire.

Our PG journey began in Bhopal, the heart of Madhya Pradesh., a beautiful city of lakes, forests, and rivers. The Gandhi Medical College stood with quiet dignity, and right across from the hostel stretched a serene lake, reflecting the peace we were about to be robbed of.

Orthopaedics wasn't a smooth ride. It was a battlefield—and I had just been drafted." In fact, looking back, it feels like one of the most defining and challenging achievements of my life. Even today, when I close my eyes, I can vividly recall those early days of my post-graduation—it was a phase that tested my limits, broke me down at times, but ultimately rebuilt me into the doctor I am today.

I was fortunate to join Gandhi Medical College, a reputed government institute, where I not only pursued my passion but also met some of the most genuine souls—friends who were intelligent, humble, and remain close to me even today. Our hostel was located just in front of a large lake. I still remember the view—the calming water gently reflecting the sky, as if offering a moment of peace before the chaos of each day began.

Each Day Began

May 31st—our first day in the department. Nine of us PG candidates walked in, a mix of excitement and nervous anticipation etched across our faces. Our first posting: Casualty.

I still remember the room—Small. Glass-walled. Packed to suffocation. The month of May had brought unbearable heat. The air was thick with tension, filled with cries of pain, the rustling of case sheets, and the sharp smell of antiseptics.

At the center of it all stood a single table, overflowing with X-rays, patient files, and scribbled notes. Around it, seniors moved with machine-like focus—applying slabs, reducing fractures, dressing wounds. Their coats clung to their backs, drenched in sweat, but they didn't pause.

Patients moaned. Some yelled. Others looked at us with a mix of desperation and anger after hours of waiting. It was chaos. Raw, real, unfiltered. And right there, in that storm of suffering and urgency, our journey truly began.

For sincere, academic students like us, who had imagined orthopaedics to be neatly organized operations and clinical cases, this was a shock. A few of us, including myself, seriously questioned if we had made the right choice.

That very day, one of our colleagues couldn't take it. He excused himself, citing his sister's marriage, and left. But he never returned. He wasn't the only one—over time, three candidates left the course, unable to adjust to the grind. The workload was immense. The patient flow was relentless.

And we, being fresh and inexperienced, were not yet skilled at even the basics—reductions, slab applications, interpreting emergency X-rays. Everything felt new, and everything drained us. Our day ends and night started with exhausted, both physically and mentally.

For the first five to six months, we barely had time to return to our hostel rooms, take a proper bath, or even change our aprons. Long, stained aprons, unkempt hair, and small shoulder bags became the unmistakable identity of an orthopaedic first-year resident

But slowly, something changed. We started adapting. Learning from seniors. Observing. Asking questions. Practicing. Our hands began to gain confidence, our eyes started recognizing patterns, and our minds began to accept the chaos—not as disorder, but as real-life medicine in motion.

And amidst that whirlwind, real friendships were born. Bonds formed not in air-conditioned classrooms, but in sweat-soaked scrubs, 3 AM fracture reductions, shared 20-20 biscuits and tea after night duty, and silent support during emotional breakdowns.

But amid the exhaustion, something shifted in me. We treated patients with chronic, non-healing wounds—wounds that went far deeper than skin. I began to feel their emotional suffering, their helplessness. And I realised: healing wasn't just about fixing bones. It was about connecting.

At first, all our seniors seemed aggressive, even intimidating. But gradually, I understood—they weren't harsh; they were hardened by responsibility. Over time, I learned that a doctor's behaviour could often do what medicine couldn't—it could heal the human spirit.

Surprisingly, this was the first phase of my life where I began to feel truly alive. There was love in my life. A stipend began to flow in, giving me the first taste of financial freedom. I was growing—not just as a doctor, but as a person.

There was one shadow that had loomed over me since childhood Cluster headaches. They had haunted me relentlessly since Class 8. The pain was savage—like a hammer pounding the left side of my skull. Even the slightest sound felt like an explosion. My eyes would tear up. My nose would run. And all I could do was curl up and endure it in silence.

But strangely—miraculously—during those early PG days, something changed. Despite sleeping barely two or three hours a night, constantly on my feet, mind always racing between patients and emergencies... the headaches began to fade. By the end of nine months—They were gone. Completely.

I don't know if it was the adrenaline, the purpose, or the sheer mental resilience that overtook the pain. But I had learned something profound: Sometimes, when the mind is deeply anchored to meaning, the body forgets its pain. and never returned. Perhaps pain, when faced head-on, eventually bows down.

And for the first time in my life—I bought a vehicle. Not just any vehicle. My dream bike: a black Bullet Electra 350. Before this, I had never even owned a bicycle. Now, I rode through the fresh morning air along Bhopal's VIP Road, beside the glistening lake. It became a sacred ritual—a time of strength, solitude, and renewal.

From long shifts in the ward to long rides by the lake, orthopaedics wasn't just shaping my hands—it was shaping my soul. This wasn't just the start of a career. This was the start of transformation—from textbook knowledge to practical wisdom, from theoretical medicine to healing in its rawest form. And despite the overwhelming start, I know now—this is where I truly became a doctor.

A Reflection: More Than Just Degrees

If there's one thing I wish I had learned earlier—not just in orthopaedics, but in my entire medical journey—it's financial management. Today, I don't regret the hardships. I don't regret the long nights or the countless sacrifices. But one thing I *do* regret is that we were never taught how to manage money, how to save, how to plan for the future, or how to dream beyond a secure government job.

Our stipend back then was more than enough to survive. I would send some money home, pay the EMI on my education loan, and the rest? It disappeared. I can't even recall where it went. Because if you're not measuring, not tracking, not being financially accountable—you're not building your future. You're just floating.

Like most of us, I was conditioned to believe that success meant collecting degrees and eventually landing a secure government job. Risk-taking wasn't part of our vocabulary. No one told us we could dream bigger.

Now, as I write this book, I want to speak directly to every young doctor, medical student, or anyone chasing a professional dream: A job alone will not secure your future. You must secure *yourself*. You must build a *brand—yourself* as the brand. You must unlearn the false comfort society teaches: that safety lies in salary.

What we should begin doing—starting from the moment you read this paragraph—is what I'll explore in the chapters ahead. Because a powerful life isn't built just in operation theatres or classrooms—It's built through awareness, vision, and the courage to rewrite your own path.

The Moment My Mindset Changed

After the sleepless storm of first year. I slowly returned to myself—to my inner world. I revived my Miracle Morning routine: I woke up at 4 AM, read spiritual and motivational books, listened to powerful videos and immersing myself in the journeys of those who had built legacies—Warren Buffett, Bill Gates, and many others, studied peacefully, and hit the gym every day. And something within me began to transform and their stories didn't just inspire me—they shattered the mental ceiling I had unknowingly built around myself.

Until then, my world revolved around studies, duties, and the idea of landing a secure job. But through their words, I realized something profound: Success isn't about collecting degrees. It's about creating impact. It's not about survival. It's about vision.

From that point onward, I stopped thinking like just a student or a government servant in the making. I started thinking like a *creator*, an *architect of my future.* I began to dream—not just only being a good doctor, but of building something of my own. An empire. A legacy.

9

The Turning Point: From Expertise to Vision

It was no longer just about treating patients—it was about transforming lives and redefining what it meant to be a doctor.

"The best way to predict your future is to create it." – ***Abraham Lincoln***

"Success depends upon previous preparation, and without such preparation, there is sure to be failure." – ***Confucius***

The final months of my Senior Residency were not just an academic wrap-up—they marked the beginning of something deeper: the transition from becoming an expert to becoming a visionary. It was no longer just about mastering orthopaedic procedures; it was about choosing the life I wanted to live beyond the operation theatre.

One of the most impactful pieces of advice I ever received came from Dr. Sanjiv Gaur Sir, a mentor I deeply respect—who taught us orthopaedics not just as a subject, but as a way of life. He said something I still carry in my heart: "Choose your specialty not just by your interest, but according to your final destination—where you see yourself living your life, raising your family, and building your future."

This struck a deep chord. For most of us, especially doctors, the focus remains so tightly locked on securing a degree, a seat, a rank—that we often forget to pause and ask, Where do I actually want to live? What kind of life do I want to build, and with whom?

- Decide your settlement location almost 5–6 months before finishing your bond or senior residency—not after it's over.
- Choose one of the two:
  1. Your native place, where your roots, network, and emotional anchors lie. If it's decent enough for livelihood and education, this choice offers stability.
  2. The place where you did your MBBS or PG (or both)—because by now, you've already built relationships, know the system, and understand the social and professional environment.

"A tree is strongest when it grows where its roots run deep." ***-Unknown***

When I started talking to seniors across the country, I began to notice a clear pattern. Those who had made conscious choices—carefully considering location, long-term lifestyle, and future vision—were not just surviving, they were thriving. In contrast, those who chose impulsively, ignoring these crucial factors, often found themselves struggling, stuck in environments that didn't align with their goals or personality. Some, after years of dissatisfaction, even relocated—finally discovering peace, purpose, and progress.

Ironically, I made the same mistake. But that mistake became my greatest teacher. And it is this lesson I now share with you—so you can make your choices with clarity, not regret. It's not about choosing a "big city" or a "small town." It's about choosing what's aligned with your long-term life plan. If you dream of Tier 1 or Tier 2 cities, then:

- Be ready to upgrade—get decent fellowships or super-speciality exposure.

- Don't fear competition. You're not there to compete; you're there to grow.

"Don't race others—run your own race and focus on getting better every single day." – ***Anonymous.***

Big cities have big opportunities. But to stand out, you must level up—not only clinically, but also in communication, management, empathy, and even personal branding.

I would highly recommend:

- Training at high-volume centres in metro cities or even overseas fellowships, if possible.
- These experiences expand your clinical mind and your cultural horizon.
- You not only learn treatment—but also how to manage patients, staff, life, and finances in a modern, systematic way.

"Travel is more than seeing new places. It's seeing with new eyes." – ***Marcel Proust***

What I learned in this phase was: If you don't build your dream, someone else will hire you to build theirs. And most importantly—no one teaches us how to plan a future, we must take that responsibility ourselves. We'll dive deeper into this transition from doctor to magnate, from service to strategy, in Section 2 of this book.

But remember this for now: "A wise person doesn't wait for the perfect time to start—they create it." Your decisions today are the blueprint of your tomorrow.

SECTION 2: BECOMING THE DOCTOR WITHIN

Success in medicine begins with mastering the mind. The real transformation, however, comes from evolving your role from a service provider to a strategist.

10

Identify Yourself First

The moment I stopped copying others and started understanding myself, everything began to change.

"A ship in harbor is safe, but that is not what ships are built for."– ***John A. Shedd***

"Clarity is the foundation of greatness."– ***Robin Sharma***

You might expect me, as a diplomate, to tell you that success starts with changing who you are. But that's only partially true. There are two ways to become a Doctor Magnate:

1. Understand and slightly evolve your behavior, if needed.
2. Accept yourself completely—and build a life aligned with your natural strengths.

Let's break this down with a real example. If you consider yourself an introvert, you can still build a thriving, respected medical career. You might choose specialties like radiology or pathology, where direct patient interaction is limited.

But if you choose to stretch your comfort zone, you can master the art of communication and become an interventional radiologist or hemato-oncologist—fields that blend deep technical knowledge with direct patient care.

Some people naturally crave a peaceful, quiet life. Others thrive on challenge, visibility, and dynamic work. The truth is—both types can become a Doctor Magnate. The path may differ, the timeline may vary, but success remains possible for each.

"The journey of becoming a doctor doesn't begin with MBBS—it begins with the subjects you choose in school." Whether you chose biology, mathematics, commerce, or the arts—your inclinations, beliefs, and early decisions shaped where you are now. And even if medicine wasn't your personal choice—maybe your parents or peers influenced it—once you're here, don't live in regret. Live with purpose.

Why? Because medicine is one of the only professions that cannot be replaced. And yet—it is also one of the few professions that can expand into nearly every other field. A doctor can:

- Start a healthcare business.
- Learn IT skills and build software solutions.
- Become a medico-legal expert or pursue a law degree.
- Enter politics through social work and community involvement.
- Write books, teach, or motivate others.

But engineers, lawyers, or businessmen cannot simply become doctors. They'd have to return to school, pass tough exams, and spend years in hospitals. You, as a doctor, hold the strongest base of all.

So the question is: Who are you, really? Introvert or extrovert, quiet or vocal, peaceful or driven—it doesn't matter. What matters is that you identify yourself clearly and design a path that honors that identity. "Know thyself—and build wisely."

Some of the best real-life examples from my own journey are my friends Arvind and Sunil Mishra. Both were intelligent and had access to the resources needed to crack medical entrance exams. But the one thing they lacked was the willingness to stretch beyond their comfort zones. They believed that exams like PMT were too tough, and that only a few "exceptional" students could make it. This belief system became a self-fulfilling prophecy. Not because they couldn't do it—but because they never really tried with full intensity. They didn't step out of the zone where comfort ruled over ambition.

On the other hand, I witnessed hundreds of students from modest or even difficult backgrounds who focused only on their goal and believed with all their heart that *"one seat is mine."* That unshakable belief—not just intelligence or coaching—is what created results.

I consider myself fortunate to have studied at Allen, one of the best coaching institutes in India. But that's not the only path to success. I remember a fellow batchmate from MBBS—Vipin Jain. He never went to any coaching class. Yet, he cracked the exam on his own and later made an even bolder move—he left medicine and became an IAS officer. He redefined what it means to identify your own strengths and act accordingly.

The moral is simple: It's not about what you have. It's about how badly you want it—and what you're willing to do for it.

"Your comfort zone is a beautiful place—but nothing ever grows there."

For all those who have entered medical college — start enjoying the journey, no matter what your personality is. Whether you're introverted or outspoken, studious or social — medicine welcomes all, but only rewards those who stay committed to the path. But don't follow the wrong path — like skipping lectures, avoiding postings, or ignoring post-lecture tests. That may feel like fun or rebellion at first, but it will haunt you later.

If you feel that medicine isn't your true calling and want to pursue something else — like becoming an IAS officer or entering healthcare administration — it's okay. But don't make a complete 360° shift and neglect your MBBS subjects entirely. I've seen many students in my own college start preparing for UPSC from the 1st professional year with great enthusiasm, only to fail both the medical and civil paths because of a lack of planning and balance.

The wise approach is this:
→ Study your MBBS subjects sincerely.
→ If you want to transition into UPSC or MBA, start preparing strategically, not impulsively.
→ Finish your MBBS with a decent score — it gives you credibility and opens many doors.
→ You can still become an IAS, a hospital CEO, a health tech founder, or a policy leader — but build your base first.

This book, *Doctor Magnate*, isn't just about becoming rich or famous. It's about growing through small, smart decisions. It's about recognizing that your past doesn't define you — your next step does. We don't have to make all the mistakes ourselves to learn. Learn from winners — and yes, learn from those who didn't make it too. I never use the word "loser" — it's not in my dictionary — but some stories serve as reminders of what not to do.

"What you do makes a difference, and you have to decide what kind of difference you want to make." —***Jane Goodall***

The medical field is not one-size-fits-all. Your personality shapes your success far more than you think.

Let's break it down:

1. The Comfort-Seeker (Low Risk, Low Stress, Fixed Routine)
   If you are someone who values comfort, routine, and a risk-free lifestyle, then choose a branch or job that gives you fixed duty hours and minimal unpredictability.
   - Ideal Path: Government job, medical college faculty, diagnostic specialties (Radiology, Pathology, Microbiology).
   - These roles offer balance, stability, and peace of mind without needing to hustle like an entrepreneur.
2. The Dedicated Workhorse (High Effort, Low Risk-Taking)
   If you are hard-working, sincere, and deeply committed, but not

keen to take risks or handle business stress — then a corporate hospital is the right fit.

  - Ideal Path: Full-time consultant in reputed hospitals where infrastructure and patient flow are already established.
  - Focus on skill mastery, long-term reputation, and steady career growth without ownership stress.

3. The Doctor Magnate Personality (Hard Working, Risk-Taker, Stress-Resilient)
   If you are highly driven, can handle stress, ready to take risks, and have a strong desire to create impact — you are made for building something big.
   - Ideal Path: Start your own clinic in a small town and scale it. Or, research your options and start a unique setup in a metro or tier-2 city.
   - You can create a hospital, a diagnostic chain, or a health-tech platform.
   - These doctors don't just follow systems. They create ecosystems.

"The path to prosperity begins where your personality meets purpose."

Remember, the last two types may live within the same person. Some doctors start risk-averse and grow into visionaries. Others begin boldly but become more balanced with time. There's no fixed formula — only the right fit for *you*.

Let Your Nature Choose the Right Specialty

"Know thyself, and you'll know where you shine best."

In the race of postgraduate medical selection, one truth remains constant: No matter which branch you choose, you'll have to study hard. But what many students overlook is aligning their natural personality with the right specialty.

The Ideal Strategy:

Aim high. Prepare as if you're going to get the topmost institute of India—AIIMS, PGI, JIPMER, BHU. This way, you'll never have to compromise on either subject or college. But while dreaming big, also understand yourself.

Match Your Nature to Your Branch:

1. **Aggressive, Action-Oriented, Frontliner (Low initial communication skill):**
    - **Best fit:** Surgery, Orthopaedics, ENT, Obstetrics & Gynaecology and Anaesthesia
    - These branches demand physical stamina, decision-making under stress, and running around to get things done.
    - Communication can be developed later, but courage is innate.
2. **Calm, Good Communicator, Not Physically Aggressive but Studious:**
    - **Best fit:** Medicine, Pediatrics, Dermatology.
    - These require deeper knowledge, strong doctor-patient relationships, and long-term care responsibility.
3. **Quiet, Peace-Seeking, Private Personality – Not Interested in Patient Crowds or Physical Hardship:**
    - **Best fit:** Radiology, Pathology, Microbiology. These specialties allow a more back-end role in healthcare with lesser direct patient load.

Special Note on Dermatology:

- It's a clinical branch but often chosen for lifestyle balance.
- A good personality and appearance may offer extra benefit in private practice.

- Best suited for charming, confident, and aesthetically aware doctors.

Doctor Magnate Tip:

Be brutally honest with yourself. Don't follow trends. Follow your temperament.

You can always upgrade skills, but you can't change your core nature easily. Let your personality guide your path—and success will follow.

The Nature Within – A Story That Teaches Everything

How your nature can decide the best—or the worst—for you.

This story is not borrowed. Not imagined. Not something I read or heard from someone else. It was unfolding right in front of me. Parallel to my own journey. It was the counselling day. Like every medical aspirant, I was anxious, alert, and constantly calculating—figuring out what branch to choose, what options to leave, and how a single choice would shape the next decades of life.

In that moment, the counselling hall wasn't just a place. It was a battlefield of dreams. One candidate was sitting beside me. He had a better rank than mine. Out of curiosity and maybe brotherhood of stress, I asked him, "Which branch are you choosing?" He replied, "Orthopaedics."

Now, here's the interesting part: I already knew this candidate. In the first round of counselling, he had taken MD Medicine from Gwalior. In the second round, he had shifted to Pediatrics. And now, in the third round, he was sitting next to me, about to opt for Orthopaedics.

I told him, "One seat of Dermatology is going to be vacant." His eyes widened. Without wasting a second, he dialed his mother to ask if he should switch to Dermatology. But time doesn't always wait for emotion. Before he could reach a decision—his name was called. No time left to consult. No time left to reflect.

And just like that, he stood up... and chose Orthopaedics at Gandhi Medical College, Bhopal. What do you think happened? Did he succeed in Orthopaedics? Did he become a brilliant bone surgeon? He joined with me. We worked side by side. Same environment. Same duty hours. Same chaos, same cuts, same crises. We walked the same path. Struggled through the same sleepless nights.

But there's one truth I learned the hard way—your inner nature always speaks. The real tragedy is when you don't listen. He wasn't naturally aggressive, nor was he drawn to physical toil. But in the race for top branches, Orthopaedics looked like the obvious choice—after all, it was what the toppers were choosing. So, he followed the trend, ignoring the quiet voice inside that kept whispering something else.

He entered Orthopaedics with ambition in his eyes... but restlessness in his soul. He worked hard, pushed through, and kept going—for five, six long months. Then suddenly... he vanished.

Gone. Left the department. Left Orthopaedics. A whole year wasted—after already dropping a year before PG. A double blow.

And then? He started all over again. Appeared for NEET PG once more. This time, he got Diploma in Paediatrics. And strangely—it fit. His nature—calm, gentle, composed—finally found its place. But imagine—once having MD Medicine in hand, and ending up with a Diploma. Not because of intelligence, not because of effort—But because he didn't know himself.

He was torn between expectations and reality—walking a path that wasn't truly his. On paper, he had everything. But inside, he was at war with himself. And when there's no alignment between your nature and your path, even success feels suffocating. His story became a turning point for me.

"Success is not the key to happiness. Happiness is the key to success. If you love what you are doing, you will be successful."– **Albert Schweitzer**

Your rank may give you options. But only clarity will give you peace. Your inner voice isn't just a guide—it's your compass. Ignore it, and even the best seat will feel like a cage. Follow it, and even the smallest branch can become a tree of destiny.

Before the forms and the choices, before the college and the branch, before NEET and coaching...You must sit with yourself. And listen. Because the worst choices aren't made by poor students. They're made by confused minds.

11

Be Grateful for All Your Past

Every scar, every stumble, every sleepless night—was silently shaping the doctor I was destined to become.

"Sometimes, not getting what you want is a wonderful stroke of luck."– ***Dalai Lama***

"I am grateful for all my problems. After each one was overcome, I became stronger and more able to meet those that were still to come."–***James Cash Penney***

At that time, I didn't feel grateful at all. I felt... disappointed. Honestly, heartbroken. I had completed my MBBS from MGM Medical College, Indore—my home turf. Naturally, I wished to pursue my MS Orthopaedics from the same institute. Familiar surroundings. Known mentors. My city.

In the first round of PG counselling, both I and a batchmate with a slightly better rank got seats in Gandhi Medical College, Bhopal. But in the second round, he got upgraded to MGM Indore. I waited with hope. I kept checking lists, waiting for a miracle. But that miracle never came. I remained in Bhopal.

I remember the disappointment I carried back then. I had dreamt of being in my home college again, with familiar faces and the comfort of belonging. And now, that door was closed. But life has its own counselling rounds. Not based on marks. But on maturity and hindsight. Because now—after completing my MS Orthopaedics from Bhopal—I know something with certainty: God didn't reject my wish. He upgraded my growth.

Bhopal turned out to be one of the best institutes I could have ever learned from. The city itself—so calm, so green, so full of nature—had a healing rhythm to it. But even more than the city itself, it was the mentors who truly shaped my journey. One such mentor was Dr. Sunil Rajan Sir—an exceptional surgeon, teacher, and guide. Before the counselling process, he shared a thought that stayed with me:
"Choose a place where you can learn everything—from the basics like crush injuries and amputations to advanced procedures like arthroplasty. Don't chase glamour, chase growth." It wasn't just advice—it was a deeper truth about medical learning and professional evolution. His words helped me focus not on the reputation of a place, but on the kind of exposure and hands-on experience that would mold me into the doctor I aspired to become.

Dr. Sunil Rajan Sir had himself completed his MS from GMC Bhopal and was a respected faculty member at MGM Indore and now mentoring new young orthopaedic surgeons in Indore. He spoke from experience and wisdom—he knew where meaningful training could be found. I'm grateful I paid attention—not always directly, but often indirectly, through the subtle nudges of destiny. His words, and his presence, became part of the inner compass that guided me during that crucial phase.

From those chaotic emergency duties, to the calm yet intense focus inside the operation theatres...From handling trauma cases to watching live surgeries with fine precision...From struggling residents to wise mentors...Bhopal shaped me. Built me. Broke me. And rebuilt me stronger.

And today, I say it with a full heart: Be grateful. For what didn't happen. For what did. For what you feared. For what you received. Because behind every detour, there's a deeper direction. Not getting Indore didn't destroy my journey. It upgraded it.

The Power of Gratitude

It was during one of the most emotionally and financially challenging phases of my journey that I discovered the true power of gratitude. There was no sudden miracle or overnight change. But something shifted within me—a deep realization that no matter how difficult life may seem, there is *always* something to be thankful for.

From that time onward, I made it a conscious habit to practice gratitude—for everything. Whether it was good or bad, easy or hard, joyful or painful—I began thanking God. I started acknowledging the blessings that were already present in my life: a roof over my head, a beating heart, the chance to chase my dream of becoming a doctor, friends who stood by me, mentors who guided me, even challenges that strengthened me.

And something magical began to happen. The more I expressed gratitude, the more life seemed to give me. Opportunities appeared, people offered help, energy returned, and even in hardships, I found hidden lessons and unexpected blessings. It was as if the universe—or perhaps God—was saying, *"Now that you truly value what you have, you are ready to receive more."*

"Gratitude turns what we have into enough, and more." – ***Aesop***

I started keeping a Gratitude Journal—a simple notebook where I wrote down every small and big thing I was thankful for: "Today I studied for 6 hours without losing focus." "Someone smiled at me on the road and I felt seen." "I had a full plate of food, thanks to my friend." "I'm healthy. I'm alive. I still have a chance."

Even on days when it felt like everything was going wrong, I pushed myself to write *at least three things* I was grateful for. At first, it felt mechanical, but soon it became my fuel. Writing, reflecting, and revisiting my journal regularly showed me the bigger picture: Life had given me far more abundance, joy, and progress than pain or difficulty.

When we zoom out from daily irritations and look at life through the lens of gratitude, we realize how *rich* we already are. Gratitude is not just an emotion—it's a mindset, a spiritual practice, and even a strategy for success.

Make this a habit:

Write daily. Reflect weekly. Revise monthly. Your Gratitude Journal will become your personal proof of progress, and your strongest source of peace during storms. Because in the end, the more we thank God, the more we receive from Him—not just in material terms, but in strength, peace, clarity, and blessings we never even asked for.

"When you drink water, remember the source." – ***Chinese Proverb***

Gratitude keeps us humble. It reminds us that we are not alone. And it brings us closer to the divine rhythm of life, where giving thanks opens the doors to more joy.

More Advantages of Practicing Gratitude

Gratitude is not just a feel-good emotion—it's a powerful mindset shift that affects every aspect of life. Here's what I discovered over time:

1. **Reduces Stress and Anxiety**

When you focus on what's going well instead of what's lacking, your mind shifts from a state of worry to a state of peace. Gratitude brings calmness, helping you tackle problems with a clear and balanced mind.

2. **Improves Sleep**

Grateful thoughts before sleeping lead to a peaceful mind. Studies show people who write what they're thankful for sleep faster and deeper.

3. **Strengthens Relationships**

When you express appreciation—even silently—for the people around you, you begin to notice their positive qualities more. This reduces unnecessary conflicts and increases emotional connection.

4. **Boosts Self-Worth**

Gratitude lets you recognize your progress and victories, however small. Over time, this builds self-confidence and a sense of fulfillment.

5. **Magnifies Positivity**

You attract more of what you focus on. If you constantly acknowledge the good, your brain becomes wired to find even more good in every situation.

Tricks to Make Gratitude a Daily Habit

Sometimes, life gets busy or overwhelming, and we forget to pause and reflect. These simple methods helped me stay consistent:

1. **Gratitude Journal (2-Minute Ritual)**

Every night before sleeping, write down 3 things you're grateful for that day. Keep the journal beside your bed. No overthinking—just short, honest entries.

2. **Gratitude Reminder on Phone**

Set a daily alarm or notification at a fixed time (e.g., 9 PM) titled: "What went right today?" It will gently push you to reflect, even on hectic days.

3. **Gratitude Anchors**

Link gratitude to daily habits. For example: While brushing your teeth, recall one person you're grateful for. While drinking tea/coffee, think of one thing that made you smile today.

4. **Thank a Person Weekly**

Once a week, send a message or call someone just to say thank you for something they've done. You'll feel a deep emotional lift—and so will they.

How Gratitude Emotionally Transforms You

I didn't realize this at first, but slowly, gratitude reshaped my entire emotional landscape.

- **From Victim to Victor:**
  I stopped asking "Why me?" and started asking "What is this teaching me?" That shift made me emotionally resilient.
- **From Restless to Content:**
  I stopped chasing what others had and started appreciating what I had. My sense of inner peace grew.
- **From Scarcity to Abundance:**
  I no longer felt I was "lacking" anything. Even if my bank account was low, my heart was full.

- **From Fear to Faith:**
  Gratitude increased my trust in God's plan. I realized He had already carried me through so much—and would continue to.

*"Gratitude is not only the greatest of virtues, but the parent of all the others." – **Cicero***

Final Thought:

Gratitude doesn't mean ignoring pain. It means choosing to see the light—even when it's dim. It's a gentle reminder that life, despite its flaws, is a precious gift. So, my dear reader—if you do just one thing after reading this chapter, let it be this: Start thanking life for what you already have. And watch how life gives you more reasons to say thanks.

12

Feel Like the Best in the World

Not arrogance—but unshakable belief. That self-image creates energy and results. Practice It Like a Habit

"Act as if it were impossible to fail." – ***Dorothea Brande***

"Whether you think you can, or you think you can't—you're right."— ***Henry Ford***

We often hear people say, *"I'm just a backbencher,"* or *"I'm an average student — topping is not for me.* "These phrases sound casual, even harmless. But in reality, they're mental habits formed early in life — and once they take root, we begin to live by them without even realizing it. And then one day, we wake up and ask ourselves: *Why have I never felt truly capable?*

The truth is — this average mindset is not your identity, it's just a belief you've been repeating for too long. But the best part? Even if we didn't learn the mindset of excellence in our past — there's *nothing* stopping us from learning it now. Believing that *"I am the best"* isn't arrogance — it's a declaration of potential. It's a mindset shift from mediocrity to mastery. It doesn't mean you're perfect.

It means you've decided to show up with full power — every single day "Mediocrity and greatness are both habits — the only difference is which one you practice consistently." We've seen time and again that

even so-called "average" or "backbench" students don't always fail in life. Many rise and do wonders. But imagine if they had believed in their best right from the start? Imagine if you, right now, commit to executing your best — in everything you do — for the rest of your life.
You'll not only succeed — you'll become a path-shower for others. A creator. A leader. A light. So how do you practice the feeling of being the best? It's simple — but only if you do it consistently and consciously:

- Every morning, stand in front of the mirror and say out loud: *"I am the best."*
- While walking to your hospital, office, or college: *"I am the best."*
- When you return home, after your full day of effort: *"I am the best."*
- Before starting any new project or task: *"I am the best."*
- And most importantly, after completing any task — big or small: *"I am the best*
- Say it with emotion. Say it with belief. Say it until your mind and body start aligning with that energy.

Because what you affirm repeatedly becomes your reality.

There was a time when comparing myself to others used to fill me with an inferiority complex. That feeling became the biggest shackle holding me back. I would think about my batchmates—how they had regular tuition, separate study rooms filled with new books, even a study table with a reading lamp. I convinced myself that these were the things that made them toppers in the final exams.

But everything changed when I moved from Vivekanand School to Boys School. My studies were just average, yet I started performing better than most. And then something incredible happened—my teachers noticed. They told me, *"You can top the board exams. You can get selected in PMT."* That was the turning point.

Slowly, I discovered the power of autosuggestion—a deep belief that I am capable, I am worthy, I am the best. It wasn't ego. It wasn't arrogance. It was a quiet, unshakable belief that I am meant to win, no matter how hard the road.

As the old proverb says, "*Comparison is the thief of joy.*" The moment I stopped looking at what others had, and started focusing on what I could become, everything began to shift. From that moment on, I carried that mindset into everything I did. Even while writing this book, I truly believe it will become one of the best books—not just for doctors, but for anyone seeking meaning, clarity, and purpose in life.

Believing that you're the best, facing your struggles head-on, and maintaining a mindset that's both tough and calm—that is the real key to achieving anything, no matter which field you belong to.

The Hanuman Realization

There comes a moment in life when you realize that everything you've been searching for outside has always been within you. It's a realization that shifts your entire being — very much like Hanuman's awakening. He always had divine strength, yet it remained hidden until he remembered who he truly was. That moment of remembrance transformed him from a humble devotee into an unstoppable force of faith and power.

We are no different. The instant you begin to believe — truly believe — that greatness is possible for you, something inside changes. Your thoughts sharpen. Your focus deepens. Your habits begin to align with the person you aspire to become. You start thinking, acting, and living like the version of yourself who has already achieved the dream — whether that's cracking a top medical exam, building a revolutionary idea, or leading a life of impact and abundance.

From that point onward, life begins to respond differently. The right people appear. Unexpected doors open. Circumstances start arranging themselves in your favor — as if the universe recognizes your decision and starts collaborating with you. But belief alone isn't enough; you must walk the path with courage. Every challenge will test your faith, patience, and clarity. Yet when you stay rooted in that inner Hanuman energy — that quiet, unshakeable strength — doubt loses its power over you. You begin to move forward with calm confidence, knowing that your purpose is stronger than any obstacle.

As your mindset evolves, your entire being starts to align. You feel more alive — every sense tuned to your purpose. You stop drifting through your days and begin to live with intent. You wake up with clarity. You choose discipline over distraction. Time no longer feels wasted; every moment becomes a meaningful step toward the future you're creating.

And even when life throws you into uncertainty — when mistakes happen, or progress feels slow — remember this: your best self is never lost. It's still within you, waiting to rise again. Don't label your struggles as failures. See them as part of your transformation. Every setback holds a lesson, every fall builds strength.

Your best version isn't defined by success alone — it's defined by resilience. It's the part of you that stands up after every storm, stronger, wiser, and more determined. That is your true power — the divine spark that, once remembered, makes you unstoppable.

The Complete "I Am the Best" Process: Beyond Affirmations

1 . Affirm with Emotion, Not Just Repetition

Saying "I am the best" isn't about mechanical repetition. It's about feeling it. Say it with power, smile while saying it, believe it as you would believe a truth about your name or your birthday. The more emotion you add, the faster your mind accepts it as reality.

2. **Visualisation Practice**

Before sleeping or early in the morning, close your eyes for 2–3 minutes and visualize yourself succeeding at your highest level — whether it's performing surgery, leading a team, cracking a tough exam, or creating something big. See yourself as the best. Act it out in your mind. Visualization + affirmation creates a stronger belief loop.

3. **Body Language of the Best**

Your body should carry the energy of your affirmation. Stand tall, shoulders relaxed but confident, Walk with purpose, Make eye contact, smile often, When your body reflects your inner belief, your subconscious begins to align faster.

4. **Micro Excellence**

Start doing small tasks with full focus and pride. Whether it's writing notes, cleaning your space, making your bed, or responding to messages — do them with excellence. Excellence in small things builds the mindset of "I am the best" from the ground up.

5. **Detach from Comparison**

Being the best doesn't mean being better than others. It means being your highest self — today, better than yesterday. Celebrate your growth, not just results.

6. **Positive Association**

Spend time (even digitally!) with people, books, videos, or mentors who carry high energy and confidence. Your environment feeds your belief system. Choose wisely.

Final Thought

"I am the best" is more than just a phrase — it's a way of living. It's about carrying excellence in your attitude, your actions, and your thoughts — no matter where you start from. Yes, life will challenge you. Yes, there will be moments of doubt. But in those moments, when you still choose to believe in your greatness — that's when transformation begins. Speak it. Feel it. Live it. The world listens to those who believe in themselves before anyone else does.

13

Building a Wall Against Negativity

Not every opinion deserves space in your mind — especially when it's rooted in fear, failure, or frustration.

"He who walks with the wise grows wise, but a companion of fools suffers harm." — ***Proverbs 13:20***

"If you listen to the crowd, you'll never reach the finish line." — ***African Proverb***

Whenever you join a new company, institute, or find yourself in a new group or gathering, you'll notice something — there are always a few people who are deeply frustrated with life. They talk like they've given up already. They'll tell you, either directly or indirectly, that dreaming big is foolish. That not everyone can become wealthy. That success is reserved for a few, and you probably aren't one of them.

These people won't just discourage you — they'll do it under the disguise of "experience" and "reality." Try sharing something positive with them, and you'll hear things like: *"You haven't seen life yet." "It's not that easy to survive out there." "Opportunities? There aren't any left."*

But here's the truth: they're not warning you. They're projecting their own limitations. They're speaking from their own fears, regrets, and missed chances. I've lived through that atmosphere.

Since childhood, I've had people around me who constantly carried negativity like a badge of honor. Looking back now, I genuinely feel surprised — *how did I manage to come out of that environment with strength, peace, and purpose?*

I remember my 11th and 12th class days so clearly. We had just two rooms in our home — one that doubled as a TV room and kitchen, and another that was used for both sleeping and studying. I was laser-focused on my goals. I didn't care who came to our house or what was happening around me — my world was my books and my dream.

But the real problem started when people got close enough to speak. Relatives would say, *"Don't study so much, your eyesight will get damaged,"* or even, *"You'll go mad if you keep reading like this."* Some of my batchmates used to laugh and call me *"Ratna"* — the Hindi term for someone who just memorizes things without understanding, implying that I was wasting time.

Even well-meaning mentors told me, *"Maths might be a better option for you."* And one random person, who had studied biology himself but never got selected and ended up doing lab work, told me straight-faced, "There's no chance of selection for MBBS. Better go with maths — you can earn money by giving tuitions. Where will you even get the money to pay MBBS fees?"

Imagine if I had listened to all of them. Imagine if I had let their fears shape my future. The truth is — if you don't learn to silence the outside noise, it will silence your inner calling. Negativity is contagious. It can cloud your vision, break your spirit, and make you question your worth. That's why it's *your responsibility* to stay away from it, no matter who it comes from.

Their doubt didn't stop me. Their words didn't break me. Because my belief was louder than their noise. Let this be your reminder: surround yourself with those who uplift, not those who unload their failures on your dreams. And if no one around you believe in your vision — be your own believer. That's more than enough.

Thank God I left that world 18 years ago. Back then, I didn't even know if I *could* avoid all that negativity — I was too young, too unsure. I didn't have the wisdom or the words to fight back. But somehow, my focus protected me. My dream became my shield. I didn't escape that world by arguing with it — I outgrew it.

And today, when I look back, I feel nothing but gratitude...because I walked away from noise, doubt, and fear — and walked into a life I believed in. "You don't owe anyone your dreams, but you owe yourself the courage to protect them."

You might think — *"Talking about all this is easy, but in real life, it's not possible."* But if you truly believe me — it's not just possible, it's 100% doable. It starts with one powerful shift: Be conscious of the environments you choose. Before deciding to join or shift to any new place — whether it's a college, institute, coaching centre, company, or even a friend group — do a proper survey. Don't just look at the name or the reputation. Observe the mindset of the people there. Ask: *Are these people dreamers or complainers? Builders or blamers?*

Because once you're inside, their energy starts shaping yours. This one step can save you from years of mental confusion and self-doubt. And if you ever feel stuck in a place that drains your energy — have the courage to walk away. Your future is too precious to be surrounded by the wrong people.

...At one point, I almost lost the hope of opening a hospital. The environment was so filled with fear and doubt that even my strong desire started shaking. I began to question myself: *"Am I too ambitious?" "Is it really practical in a place like Shahdol?" "Will I be able to manage all the risks and formalities?"*

But deep inside, a voice kept whispering — *"This is not you. You're meant to create, not to copy. You're meant to lead, not to follow."* That's when I realized something very important: I was not failing because of lack of resources — I was drowning in the energy of negativity.

No matter how skilled, visionary, or hard-working you are, if you constantly absorb the hopelessness, fear, and doubts of people around you, your mindset starts bending in that direction. Even if 90% of your circle is positive — that 10% toxic influence can corrupt your inner software, your frequency, your decision-making.

And here's the tricky part: These people don't always insult or criticize you directly. They do it in subtle, soft, "caring" tones — *"I've seen the world, it's not that easy." "This is not for everyone, only a few people make it." "Don't dream too big, life is already tough.* "They say it with a smile, but it leaves a scar.

Your future is too valuable to be designed by someone else's failure story. Ignore the noise. Follow the voice inside you. Surround yourself with positive and highly successful people. Finally, with the unwavering belief that we could make it happen, my wife and I decided to take the plunge. We didn't need a partnership with anyone else. Together, with our shared vision and positivity, we built the hospital from the ground up — on our own terms.

It wasn't easy, but we knew we had each other, and that gave us strength. Her positive mindset, her unwavering support, and our combined efforts were the fuel that kept us moving forward, even when the road seemed impossible.

We learned that true success is born from collaboration, trust, and a mindset that refuses to see obstacles — only opportunities. "When two hearts with the same vision come together, even the hardest challenges become stepping stones." "The strength of a partnership lies not just in sharing the work, but in sharing the dream."

Now, looking at the hospital we've built, I can honestly say that every bit of struggle, every second of doubt, was worth it. Because when you have a positive mindset and the right person by your side, no dream is too big, no challenge too great.

When you protect your dreams from the noise of negativity, you give them the space to fly. Negativity and setbacks are powerless — unless you give them permission to stop you.

How to Keep Yourself Away from Negativity and Step Into a Positive Life

Negativity is sneaky — it enters through news, people, and even casual conversations. Most of us don't realize how our energy gets hijacked every day. You read a newspaper filled with fear, then walk into a workplace full of complaints. Over time, this dims your light.

I felt this shift when I moved to a new city. Some people spoke only of failure and frustration. I didn't argue — I just stepped back. I chose silence over stress. Slowly, my energy returned. My focus sharpened. My joy returned. Avoiding negativity doesn't solve everything, but it protects your mind. And when your mind is free, your growth begins.

Simple but Powerful Steps to Stay Positive:

1. **Choose your company slowly.** Watch people's energy before getting close.
2. **Start your day with inspiration, not information.** Read 10 pages of a good book, not a gloomy newspaper.
3. **Don't engage deeply with negative people.** Smile, greet, move on.
4. **Work with full focus.** A busy mind is a protected mind.
5. **Surround yourself with uplifting souls.** Share efforts, not just results.
6. **Change your environment if needed.** Some places don't deserve your light.
7. **Protect your dreams.** Share them only when they're in motion — and only with believers.
8. **Speak life.** Talk as if your words shape your world — because they do.
9. **Use social media wisely.** Don't scroll into sadness.

"Speak only what you want to see grow in your life."

Negativity is loud. But positivity, when practiced consistently, is life-changing.

I am discussing it totally separate as today Social media is one of the biggest silent energy killers. If you don't control it, it will control you — and silently fill your mind with negativity, comparison, jealousy, frustration, and fear. While it can be a tool for learning and connection, it can also flood your mind with:

- Negative news
- Fake success stories
- Comparison traps
- Unnecessary gossip and drama
- Trolls and criticism

You open your feed and you are suddenly comparing your journey to someone else's highlight reel. You see negative news again and again, and your subconscious mind starts believing that the world is a dark, unfair place. If you are not careful, social media can silently drain your energy, your confidence, and your peace of mind.

Here's how you can avoid its trap:

- **Start your morning without your phone.**
  For the first 1-2 hours after waking up, avoid checking WhatsApp, Instagram, Facebook, etc.
- **Set fixed times for checking social media** — and stick to it.
  Example: Only 15 minutes after lunch, or 15 minutes in the evening — not randomly all day.
- **Unfollow or mute negative accounts** that share toxic news, fake lifestyles, or spread fear and anger.
- **Keep only learning-based apps on your home screen.**
  Move entertainment apps like Instagram or YouTube to a hidden folder far away from your main screen.

- **Use apps to track and limit your screen time.** Apps like Digital Wellbeing or Stay Free can help.
- **Fill your day with meaningful offline activities.** Read real books, meet real people, walk in nature, work deeply on your passion projects spend more time with family.
- **Remember:** You don't have to quit social media — just master it before it masters you.

"If you don't program your mind, someone else

"Birds born in a cage think flying is an illness."– ***Alejandro Jodorowsky***

"If you want to fly, give up everything that weighs you down."– ***Buddha***

Daily Positivity Ritual Checklist

(Follow this daily to stay focused, happy, and inspired)

1. Wake Up with Gratitude

Start your day by silently thanking for 3 things — your health, your family, your opportunities.

2. Avoid Phone for the First 1 Hour

No WhatsApp, no Instagram, no emails.
Instead: stretch, drink water, journal, or just sit in silence.

3. Read 10 Pages of a Positive Book

Self-help, biography, spirituality, or any book that lifts you.

4. Say Your Affirmation Loudly

"I am the best. I am focused. I am unshakable." (Repeat 3 times in the mirror)

5. Plan Your Top 3 Goals for the Day

Write them down in your diary or phone — stay on track.

6. Smile and Greet with Energy

Wherever you go — hospital, clinic, office — greet others positively.

7. Avoid Negative People and Gossip

Just say "hi" and move on. Protect your vibe.

8. Control Your Social Media Time

Check only 1–2 times per day.

Mute or unfollow negative accounts.

Follow only learning and positive content.

9. Spend 5–10 Minutes in Silence or Meditation

Evening time — reflect, breathe, and recharge your inner peace.

10. End Day with Reflection & Gratitude

Ask: "What went well today?" and "What can I do better tomorrow?"

"Positivity is not a one-time action. It's a daily discipline."

Final Thought

Negativity may be common, but it's not normal. You were not born to live in frustration, gossip, or self-doubt. You were born to shine, to build, to inspire. Be intentional about what you hear, what you read, and whom you speak to. Because your inner world shapes your outer world.

Your thoughts become your actions. Your actions create your future. Guard your mind like a sacred temple. Fill it with strength, hope, gratitude, and belief.

Remember —

The world outside you can only change when the world inside you becomes powerful. So choose wisely. Every day. Every hour. Every moment. "Don't let a few negative voices drown the fire you carry inside you."

14

The Behavior Code of a Magnate Doctor

"People may forget your treatment, but they'll remember how you made them feel."

"Humility, empathy, and kindness — let your behavior heal even before your hands do."

In my journey as a doctor, I realized one deep truth early: It's not just about diagnosing a disease or prescribing a medicine — it's about touching lives with humanity. Whenever I would meet a patient, whether young or old, critical or stable, I made a simple decision: To treat them like they were my own family member.

When I gently touched their shoulder, listened to their concerns without rushing, and smiled with genuine warmth, I often saw something miraculous happen —their pain seemed to reduce, their fears began to melt, and even before any medicine was given, they started believing they could heal. This wasn't magic. It was the invisible but powerful impact of human connection —something no prescription can replace.

Over time, I noticed that patients who felt cared for, respected, and understood often recovered faster, trusted the process more deeply, and even carried home more hope than medicine alone could offer. When you practice medicine (or any profession) with humility, compassion, and service mindset, you don't just treat a body —you uplift a soul.

Phase of My Journey that Reflects It:
From my early years of internship to becoming a consultant, this principle became my silent guide: Always touch the patient with kindness. Always listen with complete attention. Always imagine them as your own family. This approach didn't just build my practice —it built unbreakable trust, loyalty, and heartfelt blessings that no advertisement could ever buy.

"You heal not just by your hands, but by your presence, your heart, and your hunger for greatness."

A Magnate Doctor is not only a skilled physician — but a source of strength, hope, and transformation for all.

Here is the complete Behavior Code of a Magnate Doctor: Inner Character

- **Ruthlessly Hardworking:** Dedicated relentlessly to service, excellence, and discipline, even when no one is watching.
- **Always Positive:** Radiates optimism even during darkest times, believing solutions are always possible.
- **Practice Positive Self-Talk:** Affirm:
  "I am growing. I am healing. I am making a difference."
  and avoid negative inner dialogues
- **Dreams Big:** Refuses to stay small — builds visions that can transform healthcare and humanity.
- **Cool, Calm, and Polite:** Stays composed even under pressure; communicates with softness and inner authority.
- **Caring and Compassionate:** Treats every patient like a beloved family member, giving respect, time, and empathy.

Professional Excellence

- **Never Prioritizes Money Over Patient Care:** Healing comes first — everything else follows naturally.
- **Always Hungry for Knowledge:** Lifelong learner, constantly upgrading skills and understanding.
- **Enthusiastic and Eager:** Brings fresh, vibrant energy into every consultation, surgery, class, and meeting.
- **Never in a Rush:** Gives each patient full presence, deep attention, and complete dignity.
- **Master of New Technologies:** Learns and applies cutting-edge technologies to enhance patient care and outcomes.

Energy and Spirit

- **Highly Energetic and Joyful:** Infects others with happiness, optimism, and unstoppable drive.
- **Never Gets Exhausted:** Draws energy from purpose, passion, and inner fire — not just external rewards.
- **Takes Risks Boldly:** Fearlessly steps into new challenges and innovations for the greater good.
- **Protect Physical Health:** Exercise daily, eat mindfully, sleep well — your energy is your biggest asset

Social Responsibility

- **Helpful to Everyone:** Supports juniors, seniors, patients, and society without hesitation.
- **Gives Back to Society:** Actively participates in community health, education, and uplifting projects.
- **Prioritize Relationships Over Ego:** Build bonds of trust, respect, and kindness with everyone you meet

The Mental and Emotional Mastery Code

- **Never Controlled by Opinions:** Listens respectfully, but ultimately follows inner clarity and mission.
- **Emotionally Strong:** Stays calm, unshaken by criticism, failures, or temporary setbacks.
- **Happy and Relaxed Always:** Carries a relaxed, joyful spirit — knowing a calm mind produces the most brilliant solutions.

Health is the real wealth, joy is the real success, and service is the real purpose. No one can disturb your peace unless you hand them the keys to it.

Final Thought:

You were not born for frustration, gossip, or mediocrity. You were born to shine, to heal, and to uplift. Protect your energy. Guard your dreams. Choose your associations carefully. Because your inner world will always create your outer results. And remember always — you are meant to be a blessing in every life you touch.

15

The Victory Mindset

Daily habits, grit, and building mental strength.

"The real battle is not in the world around you, but in the mind within you."

"1% better every day keeps mediocrity away."

We started with big dreams. To become doctors, engineers, professionals, and builders. We fought the odds, sacrificed sleep, youth, and time with family—all to achieve something worthwhile. And one day, it happens. We make it. We arrive. We build a career. Buy the house. Drive the car. Pay for the best education for our children.

And silently, slowly, we start telling ourselves: "This is enough." But here's the truth: comfort can be a trap. It can lull us into thinking that settling is success. That a routine life of hard work and occasional vacations is the final destination. We forget the fire that got us here.

From Routine to Revelation

We wake up early. We give. We fix. We lead. We manage the chaos, the emergencies, the expectations. And when the day ends, there's barely time—or energy—left for reflection, restoration, or realignment. We may still exercise. We may still perform. But what about the *inside* work? The mindset, the clarity, the personal growth? It's not burnout that always gets us—it's self-neglect disguised as discipline.

We become so focused on being *good for others* that we forget to be *good to ourselves*. As professionals, we often confuse responsibility with fulfillment. We continue working hard, but stop thinking big. We become experts at coping, but forget how to dream again. And worst of all—we start avoiding anything that feels like an extra burden. We tell ourselves: "Now's not the time." "This is enough." "Why take more risk?"

But here's the wake-up call: This mindset doesn't lead to greatness. It leads to stagnation. Look at the world's magnates—Ambani, Adani, Elon Musk. They didn't stop after achieving comfort. They created legacy, impact, and wealth across industries. They weren't content with just winning. They kept evolving. That is the Victory Mindset.

I didn't walk into medical college with privilege or polish. I wasn't the loudest voice in the room or the most admired name on a list. But I had something deeper — a quiet dialogue with myself: *"You're not here to impress. You're here to improve.* "That inner voice wasn't built during my wins. It was trained during my wounds — like when I fractured my ankle in 2010. While the surgery healed my bone, the experience restructured my ambition. That injury didn't pause my journey — it redirected it. From a general path to a focused mission: orthopaedics.

Pain, I realized, isn't just something to manage. It's something to understand — and then transform. That wasn't the only test life sent. From facing court formalities, to losing my friend's bike, to juggling emotional tides during NEET PG prep when my mother fractured her elbow — every incident felt like a detour. But they weren't. They were directions. I didn't escape those emotions. I invited them in. I let responsibility sharpen my focus, not steal it. Victory, after all, isn't found in avoidance. It's built through alignment.

That's the victory mindset. Not a mindset of ego or emotionless drive — but one that holds both purpose and passion. It doesn't wait for the storm to pass. It anchors itself in the middle of it. Because real victory? It's not found at the finish line. It's created, moment by moment, in how you run the race.

Why Doctors Must Develop This Mindset

In medicine, we don't just treat illness — we navigate intensity. We're asked to deliver clarity in the middle of chaos, to stay focused while life moves fast and unfiltered. Surgical precision isn't enough. Academic excellence isn't enough. What sustains us — day after day, case after case — is the *mental muscle* we build. The *Victory Mindset* isn't a motivational quote — it's a survival skill. Without it, even brilliance can burn out. With it, even a struggling student can evolve into a surgeon who saves more than lives — they restore trust, dignity, and direction.

Key Lessons from the Victory Mindset

- **Believe Before Proof Appears**
  True belief starts before the results do. It's not about being delusional — it's about being *deliberate.*
- **Redefine Setbacks as Strategy**
  Rejection doesn't reduce you — it redirects you. Every closed door sharpens your focus for the one that opens.
- **Guard Your Mental Ecosystem**
  Protect your schedule, your boundaries, and your peace. Some distractions wear the mask of opportunity — learn to recognize the difference.
- **Build What Can't Be Bought**
  Discipline is invisible wealth. Clarity is currency. And resilience? That's your long-term investment.
- **Act in Alignment with Your Vision**
  Don't wait for applause. Behave like the person your goals demand — long before anyone notices.

The *Victory Mindset* won't spare you from difficulty. But it will spare you from defeat. Because in this journey — from hospital corridors to operation theaters — it's not ego that carries you. It's alignment. Not loud, not flashy — just steady. Like a pulse that never stops showing up.

The Doctor Who Refused to Expand

One day, I met a junior from medical college who is now practicing as a general physician in a small town. Our meeting was full of nostalgia—we laughed over old memories and soon drifted into discussing our current medical practices. Curious, I asked him, "Why haven't you extended your services to nearby areas?" He quickly replied, "Sir, I am already full with patients—from 8 in the morning till 11 at night. I have no time."

I gently asked, "Then why not delegate? If patients from far-off places are already coming to you, wouldn't it make sense to reach out to them with more structured systems—maybe by hiring junior doctors or opening satellite clinics?" But again, he disagreed. "No sir. I have to give sufficient time to each patient myself."

His commitment is admirable. But let's reflect for a moment: What happens in the long run? The answer is inevitable—burnout. Working from morning to late night, day after day, without systems, delegation, or expansion, leads to exhaustion. Eventually, he might either reduce the number of patients he can see or be forced to take long breaks, unintentionally affecting patient care.

This is where the Doctor Magnate mindset takes a different route. Instead of being tied down to one location and one schedule, a Doctor Magnate expands. He opens new centres, builds a hospital, and hires talented general physicians to work with him—not just for him. He creates a system where healthcare delivery continues even in his absence.

True wealth begins when your money and systems work even when you don't. That's the transition from being just a doctor to becoming a Doctor Magnate.

Reignite the Fire

It's not just about making money. It's about unlocking your full potential—not only for yourself, but for this world. It's about turning your skills, your story, and your sweat into something that outlives you. Your wealth shouldn't end with a salary. It should begin with a vision. The moment you say, "I want more—not out of greed, but out of purpose"—that's when your Victory Mindset activates.

The Daily Practice of Greatness

The Victory Mindset is not about working harder. It's about growing wiser. It's the decision to nurture your *inner world* with the same care you give your outer duties. Growth isn't a luxury for the free or the young—it's fuel for the driven. And the key is this: **get 1% better every day.** That's it. No pressure. No perfection. Just small, intentional steps that bring you *back to you*.

Success isn't a one-time act. It's a habit. And the most powerful tool to keep that victory mindset sharp and alive—daily—is your inner routine.

The New Morning Ritual

Let this be your new non-negotiable

Here are four daily tools that reignite your fire, sharpen your focus, and protect your vision:

1. Affirmation

Affirmation is speaking truth over yourself—especially when you don't feel it. It's declaring who you are becoming, not just who you were..

Say out loud: "I create wealth and opportunities with integrity and clarity." "I am a builder of impact, not just income." "Every day, I rise with purpose and passion."

Affirmations remind you of who you are becoming—not who you were. Affirmation brings you back to your identity, reminding you that you are not just a doctor, engineer, or leader—you are a human being with needs, dreams, and depth

2. Visualization

See your next level before it exists. Spend 3–5 minutes each morning *seeing* the best version of yourself. Calm under pressure. Clear in purpose. Confident and grounded. Visualization rewires your mind for possibility. It reconnects you with your inner power before the world demands your outer performance. Visualize launching that new idea. Visualize creating a hospital chain, a health-tech product, or a wellness brand. Visualize impacting communities, not just patients. Your brain follows what your heart rehearses.

3. Reading

A few pages of the right book can shift your perspective. Whether it's philosophy, psychology, leadership, or memoirs—reading daily keeps your mind fertile and fresh. Make it a habit—even if it's 5 pages a day. Because leaders who stop learning eventually stop leading. Feed your mind the way you feed your body. Read biographies of tycoons. Study business, psychology, money, leadership. Read content that stretches your thinking.

One idea from one page can shift your entire direction. When I was in 2nd year of PG I just started reading books and that helped me to see the fantastic results. Reading books can give you the solutions you need in life. You can generate an idea or you can protect yourself from any big danger.

Some of my favourite books *Rich dad poor dad by Robert Kiyosaki, Think and grow rich by Napolean Hill, How to win friends and influence people by Dale Carnegie, Business Strategy: The Brian Tracy Success Li-*

brary, The Secret by Rhonda Byrne, Power of subconscious mind by Joseph Murphy, Miracle morning by Hal Elrod, 5 AM Club and Everyday hero manifesto by Robbin Sharma and many more.

All these books empowered my decision making, my way of thinking my views for money and wealth and most importantly power of habits and discipline helped me in all possible way to transform me in to a new chapter of my life.

4. Journaling (Scribing)

Write your truth. Track your growth. Capture your insights. Every day, take 5 minutes to reflect: What did I learn today? What am I avoiding? Where can I multiply value—for me and others? Scribing brings vision into clarity.

Grit: The Engine Behind the Vision

Once you decide to reignite the fire, life will test you. Distractions. Doubts. Setbacks. That's where grit comes in. Grit is your refusal to shrink back. It says: "I've come too far to stop." "This comfort is not my ceiling." "Let's build. Let's lead. Let's multiply."

Victory Mindset: Not Just for You—For the World

Your victory isn't just personal. It's global. Every hospital you build, every system you create, every innovation you launch—it becomes a gift to society. Your mindset matters—not just for your income, but for the lives you impact. And when you grow wealth from multiple sources, when you multiply your influence—it's not selfish. It's service at scale. And every day, ask yourself: "What can I create today that didn't exist yesterday?"

Final Word: Refuse to Settle

You are not finished. You are just getting started. Victory isn't about what you have. It's about who you're becoming—and what you're building for others. The world needs your ideas. The world needs your energy. The world needs your fire. So build your house. Educate your kids. Buy the car. But don't stop there. Build a legacy. Build an empire. Build something beautiful—for this amazing world.

16

Wealth is Not a Sin

Growing up, like many middle-class kids, I inherited an unspoken rule: If you want to be good, don't talk about money. Especially if you're a doctor. "Doctors should serve." "They shouldn't chase wealth." "If they do — they're commercial. Not compassionate." It sounded noble. But over the years, I saw how that belief silently damaged people.

Brilliant doctors working endless hours, missing family weddings, sacrificing vacations —All while feeling guilty for even thinking about upgrading their lifestyle. Let me ask you —Why is it okay for an engineer or a businessman to dream of a villa, but a doctor must dream of duty only? We wear stethoscopes, not shackles. It's time we *free ourselves from this guilt.*

The Day I Broke the Mental Block

I still remember the day it hit me. I was sitting alone, going through my earnings after months of backbreaking OPDs, night duties, and emergency surgeries. Patients appreciated me. People said I was "doing great." But in reality, I was barely staying afloat. Every time there was a financial need — big or small — I felt stuck. Whether it was fixing a broken bike, buying a textbook, or helping my family during emergencies, there was always that sick feeling in my chest: "I don't have enough."

There were days I had to borrow money just to buy examination forms. Days when I skipped meals because the little I had needed to stretch across a week. Even during NEET PG prep — when I should've

been focused on studies — my mind was divided: part revision, part survival. And when someone in the family fell sick, like when my mother had her elbow fracture, it hurt to know that we couldn't immediately afford the best care. Not because we didn't love her.
But because money was always tight, tense, temporary.

It wasn't just about being poor — it was about being powerless. And that feeling? It's heavy. It drains your confidence, and slowly, it builds resentment. That's when I realized —Money may not buy happiness, but lack of it definitely adds pain. So I stopped feeling guilty for wanting more. Because I knew what it felt like to have *less than enough*. And I never wanted to feel that helpless again.

Money is Not a Distraction. It's a Tool.

I realized I didn't want wealth for status. I wanted it for freedom. Freedom to say no to burnout. Freedom to upgrade my parents' comfort. Freedom to give time — not just treatment — to patients. Freedom to build something lasting, without constantly being on call just to survive. And none of that makes me less of a doctor. It makes me more human.

The problem isn't money. The problem is the *guilt* we attach to it. As if dreaming big means you've abandoned your morals. But here's what life taught me: You can be deeply compassionate — and still be richly compensated. The two are not enemies. Your character defines your practice — not your paycheck. So to every doctor or any other professionals reading this: You don't have to choose between service and success. You can serve *with* success. You can build clinics *and* build wealth. You can save lives *and* live yours fully. Money isn't the opposite of service — it can *amplify* it.

Let's stop apologizing for wanting more. Because wealth is not a sin. Wasting your potential is. "You can serve better when you're not surviving. A doctor with abundance can heal with freedom."

I grew up thinking money was the enemy. Not because someone said it directly — but because of how it shaped our everyday life. Some days, we ate dal. Some days, just vegetables. On lean days, dinner was just roti with mustard oil and salt — and honestly, I loved it. It tasted like survival. I was still grateful, because I knew kids who didn't even get that. But even as a child, I saw something strange. My parents — two hardworking, honest people — were always in some kind of financial stress. Not because they didn't work hard. They just never learned to *think differently* about money.

They carried an invisible belief: "Having too much money must mean you did something wrong." Or, "Rich people aren't really happy anyway." So instead of building wealth, they built walls. Even when they started their own little pan shop — which had potential — there was no plan to grow it. No savings. No backup. And when money ran short, the same cycle would start again: stress, helplessness, then somehow getting by.

What hurt me the most wasn't just the struggle — it was the *mindset* behind it. At some point, my inner voice started asking, "Why are we always stuck here? Why is it always so hard?" And the only answer I could hear was: "Because we were taught that wanting more was wrong." That *earning well* meant compromising your morals. That *wealth* automatically came with guilt. But here's what life taught me: That belief is a lie. No, wealth is not a sin. Lack of it doesn't make you pure. And abundance doesn't make you corrupt.

What makes the difference is *how* you earn it. You can make money the wrong way — yes. That's always true. But it's just as true that you can make money the *right* way — with values, skill, service, and strategy. The truth is: We never saw wealthy people who were *well-rounded*. We never read their books, heard their stories, or learned how they thought.

We were taught: "Rich people have family issues." "Rich people are unhealthy." "Rich people aren't really happy." But I used to suffer from toothaches and headaches too — and I couldn't even afford proper treatment in my childhood. So what's the logic? Money doesn't eliminate problems — but it gives you options. And sometimes, options can be the difference between pain and peace.

So I made a decision. I won't carry guilt for wanting a better life. I won't pretend that being broke is noble. I won't romanticize struggle. Because telling yourself *money is evil* is often just an excuse —To avoid doing the *smart*, hard work needed to grow. Today, I believe this deeply: If your intentions are clean, your work is honest, and your heart is grounded — wealth is not just okay. It's powerful. Not to show off. Not to dominate. But to support your family. To serve your patients. To choose peace over pressure. To say yes when someone needs help — and mean it. Wealth isn't the enemy of happiness. But fear and guilt around money? That definitely is.

Think of the countless patients who can't afford good treatment. Now think — who can really help them? A rich doctor with resources, or a struggling one with just good intentions? When you earn well: You can treat poor patients free of cost, without guilt. You can upgrade your clinic or hospital with better machines. You can hire more staff, reduce your burnout, and improve quality of care. You can invest in your children's future, and still sleep well. Wealth is not a sign of greed. It's a sign of growth. Wealth with Ethics — A Doctor's New Mantra

We must rewrite the internal code of doctors: Charge reasonably, not cheaply. Serve with heart, but don't discount your worth. Learn how to invest, save, and grow — not just prescribe and operate. There's a difference between being greedy and being growth-minded. Greed takes without giving. Growth earns so it can give better.

What I've Learned Over the Years Your value is not your consultation fee. It's the transformation you create. Money gives options. And options give peace. If you don't plan wealth, burnout will plan your downfall. The happiest doctors are not the busiest — they're the balanced ones. Let Go of the Saint Syndrome

You didn't study 10+ years, sacrifice youth, and miss family festivals just to survive. You did all that to build a life — for yourself, your family, and your patients. So stop apologizing for success. Be the doctor who: Saves lives. Builds wealth. Uplifts others.

A New Identity: Doctor + Magnate. The world needs this new breed: Compassionate. Ethical. Empowered. Wealthy. The "Doctor Magnate" is not a fantasy. It's a necessity. Because one empowered doctor can: Inspire 100 more. Help 10,000 patients. Build 1,00,000 dreams. Your stethoscope and your bank balance can coexist. Your clinic and your comfort can rise together. And your heart and your wallet — both can stay full.

That's when another truth became clear to me: If Dr. B. R. Parekh hadn't built wealth, he couldn't have helped me or other students like me when I needed it the most. His financial strength didn't make him less of a doctor. It made him more impactful — not just in clinics, but in people's lives. *In my life.* He didn't just earn well — he used that wealth to lift others. The doctors I admired most — the ones who were calm in chaos, generous in crisis, joyful in their journey — they were not just healers. They were *creators* of wealth. Wealth that gave them time, freedom, reach — and peace of mind.

Think Like a Doctorpreneur, Not Just a Doctor

- **Medicine is your purpose; systems are your vehicle.**
  You've already created a hospital — now ask: How can this grow without me being physically present 24/7?
- **Create replicable models:**
  Just like Dr. Shetty scaled Narayana Health with affordable, high-volume surgeries, you can design efficient workflows, hire junior doctors, and implement tech that multiplies your reach without burning you out.

Monetize Your Expertise with Integrity

- **Go beyond OPD & surgery income:**
  Think of second-income channels aligned with your values:
    - Host webinars for young doctors.
    - Offer mentorship packages.

  - Build online courses on orthopaedic basics for general practitioners or students.
  - Start a YouTube channel demystifying joint pain, fractures, etc.
- **Remember:** You're not being "commercial" — you're being intentional. You're packaging knowledge to serve more people.

Build a Financial Mindset (Not Just a Medical One)

- **Track every rupee:** Just like you analyze X-rays, start analyzing your revenue, costs, debts, and ROI.
- **Invest smartly:** Doctors often ignore investing. Learn the basics of mutual funds, real estate, or even medical equipment leasing.
- **Create passive income:** For example, if your hospital owns land, could you lease out a pharmacy space, café, or diagnostic unit?

Scale Through People, Not Just Pressure

- **Empower your team:** Train junior doctors, empower nurses, and invest in admin who think like owners. The wealthiest doctors aren't solo heroes — they build strong second lines of leadership.
- **Build your hospital brand:** Use storytelling, your journey, and testimonials to create trust in the community. Reputation = Revenue over time.

Give with Structure, Not Just Emotion

- Like Dr. Parekh helped me — you can one day fund another Anil. So, create a "Giving Account" — 5–10% of your income strictly for charity, free surgeries, or student scholarships. This way, wealth becomes a vehicle for kindness, not guilt.

Your Mindset Shift in One Line:

"I'm not chasing money — I'm building capacity, so I can serve better, live fuller, and give bigger."

"Money is not a sin. Neglecting its power to heal, build, and give — that is."

As the journey ends here but not the strategy. I've shared more strategies on how you can take your skills to the next level in my next book, **From Stethoscope to Strategy: The Mindset, Money & Mission of a New-Age Doctor.**

I would love to hear your thoughts on this book. You can share your feedback with me at **doctormagnate2025@gmail.com**.

9 789334 448863

Printed at Repro India Ltd.